George Albemarle Bertie Dewar

In Pursuit of the Trout

George Albemarle Bertie Dewar

In Pursuit of the Trout

ISBN/EAN: 9783744791427

Printed in Europe, USA, Canada, Australia, Japan

Cover: Foto ©Andreas Hilbeck / pixelio.de

More available books at **www.hansebooks.com**

IN PURSUIT OF THE TROUT

All rights reserved

IN PURSUIT OF THE TROUT

BY GEORGE A. B. DEWAR

Author of
'The Book of the Dry Fly,' etc.

'A distant dearness in the hill,
A secret sweetness in the stream.'

LONDON
J. M. DENT AND CO.
ALDINE HOUSE
1898

Edinburgh: T. and A. CONSTABLE, Printers to Her Majesty

ACKNOWLEDGMENT

I HAVE to thank the Editors of the *Field*, *Daily Mail*, *Pall Mall Gazette*, *Longman's Magazine*, and *Chambers's Journal*, for kindly permitting me to republish some of the sketches contained in this little collection. My thanks are also due to my friend, Mr. Henry Hammans, after whose picture, painted by Mr. Buckman, the frontispiece has been etched. The scene is Bransbury, a lovely Test common. My excuse for dwelling once more on the increased wisdom of the trout, and for perhaps somewhat repeating myself, must be the great interest which is now being taken in the subject by so many anglers.

G. A. B. D.

CHAPTER	PAGE
I. OUR FRIEND ANGLING, .	1
II. A STREAM AND A GARDEN,	15
III. A HERTFORDSHIRE TROUT, .	22
IV. THE LITTLE PANG,	29
V. THE ANGLING EXCUSE,	36
VI. IN TADDINGTON DALE,	43
VII. A SEVEN-POUNDER,	51
VIII. THE UPRIGHT ANGLER,	58
IX. DIBBING WITH THE DRY FLY,	63
X. WILD EXMOOR, .	73
XI. SPLITCANE'S AWAKENING,	82

CHAPTER	PAGE
XII. A MAY DAY'S ANGLING,	90
XIII. A GREAT HATCH OF FLY,	98
XIV. THE THAMES TROUT FISHERMAN,	105
XV. CRICHMERE MEMORIES,	113
XVI. THE GREAT UNLANDED,	120
XVII. THE DARENTH IN JUNE,	130
XVIII. A QUESTION OF HEREDITY,	136
XIX. MAY-FLY DREAMS,	144
XX. A VISIT TO TROUTBRIDGE,	151
XXI. A PURIST AMONG PURISTS,	162
XXII. ON A HAMPSHIRE COMMON,	168

IN PURSUIT OF THE TROUT

CHAPTER I

Our Friend Angling

'My Lord, I shall work steadily at it when the fly-fishing season is over,' replied Dr. Paley to the Bishop of Durham's inquiry as to when he expected to place the result of one of his great literary labours in the publisher's hands. The stream of life ran more placid and even in the time of the author of the 'Evidences' than now, so that even busy men often had the leisure and opportunity to rest for a while on their oars without being haunted by the uneasy feeling that a day or a week of respite from work would be at the risk of their position, enabling an eager rival to outstrip them in the race. The stream flowed serene and measured then; but now its pace seems nearly always hurried, and sometimes headlong—a too continuous rush from source to sea. And yet even when the pace is most severe, very many men, closely engaged in arduous affairs, both public and private, are coming more and more to see that the fastest stream runs down the quickest, and that it is good to now and then allow oneself to drift out of the main current, as it were, into some quiet backwater, where energies may be repaired and strength fostered.

Various are the ways which the busy man, grown idle in order to be presently busy again with more effect, has of filling-in these precious gaps. To take, for instance, those two classes of hard-worked men, politicians and authors, with whose methods the writer happens to be more or less familiar. One leading politician is known to devote many of the golden hours, which he can snatch from State affairs, to the cycle and the golf-links; a second—whose name, I

Our Friend Angling

fancy, will occur quite readily to the reader —has been written of almost as often in connection with the cultivation of orchids at home as of railways and markets in Greater Britain; a third is perhaps unique among statesmen in the absorbing interest he is known to take in the laboratory; while a fourth might be described as equally at home in library and paddock—a scholar among sportsmen, and a sportsman in the best sense among scholars. It is the same with many of our most notable living authors, artists, scientists, and divines. The harder the brain-labour, in the case of the great majority of workers, the more ardently pursued the out-of-doors pursuit or hobby. I think I am not exaggerating in the interests of our well-loved sport when I say that one of the most active spirits and strenuous controversialists on the Bishops' bench is never happier nor more contented than when he takes his fishing-rod and book of flies and sets forth to spend a day or two by the banks of one of his native Welsh trout-streams. The sport, or, as old Walton called it, the art of angling, has indeed long been a very favourite one with hard-worked men. It has been called the Contemplative Man's Recreation, and to some extent truly so, for there are branches of angling which are essentially suited to him who desires to follow some very quiet and easy open-air occupation, which will not distract the even tenor of his thoughts. Float-fishing for perch, for instance, when not overmuch is doing beneath the surface of the stream, should decidedly tend to contemplation; while as for punt fishing, as carried on in dreamy Thames backwaters and byways, it is so peaceful as sometimes to lead, by an unconscious transition, from contemplation to gentle slumber, especially on a hot summer afternoon in a shady spot.

But if these methods of angling are more for the contemplative and very easy-going man, fly-fishing, whether for salmon, trout, or grayling, is surely well fitted for the active spirit. It would be a fairly long list that included all the well-known men of action who have been attached to fly-fishing, even commencing at the time when Nelson angled for trout in his favourite Wandle, learning to cast to and play his fish with the left arm after he had lost the right. As for the men of action in the worlds of intellect and art who have been keen followers of Walton, this little volume would be scarcely large enough to hold their names. Sir Humphry Davy the scientist, Burns the poet, Fawcett the political economist, Millais the painter, Charles Kingsley the novelist and preacher, and Chantrey the sculptor, are a few which occur to one. With Kingsley angling was something more than a recreation; it was a passion. Probably no man has done more than he to commend the pursuit of the trout to the present generation of authors and thinkers. The great pen-picture of the chalk stream in 'Yeast,' glowing with its sunset richness of colour, is almost enough in itself to make a man with imagination and a love of nature a fly-fisherman; and his 'Chalk Stream Studies' is an angling classic. Chantrey is perhaps more closely identified with the gun than the rod, owing to the immortal brace of woodcocks at Holkham, which he first shot and then carved, but he was a very keen fisherman. Scott—whose favourite method of capturing salmon would, I am afraid, hardly pass angling muster nowadays—said of him : 'We have ourselves seen the first sculptor in Europe when he has taken two salmon on the same morning, and can well believe that his sense of self-importance exceeded twenty-fold that which he felt on the production of any of the masterpieces which have immortalised him.'

In what, apart from the actual filling of the creel and the capture of heavy fish, does the rare and singular charm of angling reside ? is a question which non-anglers often desire to have definitely answered ; and it is one which sometimes not a little perplexes the keen fisherman himself who is not ready to analyse his own pleasures very closely.

Our Friend Angling

In this little volume an attempt is made to show that fly-fishing has varied delights besides that of bringing back a well-filled creel—which, however, is in itself a very pleasant ending to a day's angling, provided the walk home be not too long,—and that the scenery and freshness of the river-side can never be overlooked in our estimate of the charms of fishing. In order to see whether the views which I had ventured to more than once express in this matter were in any degree shared by other fly-fishermen, I sought the opinions of three very keen fly-fishermen, Mr. William Black, the novelist —who seems to find it quite as difficult as Kingsley did to keep the angler out of his stories!—Mr. Charles Cooper, the veteran editor of the 'Scotsman,' and Sir Edward Grey. Mr. Black found no difficulty in answering. 'I don't know anything about trout-fishing; but as regards salmon-fishing I should say that one of its chief charms was the wildness and remoteness of the scenery, and the delight of having with you one or two old friends.' If fishermen as a class are of Mr. Black's mind in regard to companionship, Byron's unkind allusion to angling as 'that solitary vice' must be regarded as totally unjustified. The angler, it is quite true, does desire seclusion from careless, curious, and unsympathetic intruders, but I question whether he is less desirous of pleasant company, sometimes even by the river-side, than is the sportsman in other provinces. Both Walton and Davy by their writings showed their companionable nature; and where, moreover, are firmer and more disinterested friendships made than at the angling inn? After a long, glorious day by the stream we anglers are fond of prattling the evening away in the cosy smoking-room. It is then that the sordid cares of life leave us for a time, and

'the boy's heart within the man
Begins to move and tremble.'

'I scarcely know,' was Mr. Cooper's reply, 'how to answer your question of "what constitute the chief charms of angling?"

I would almost as soon undertake to answer the question, "What constitutes the chief charm of a good wife?" Angling is all charms. It takes you into beautiful scenes. It cultivates in you the virtue of patience. It keeps your intellect from stagnating, for you must always be thinking of what you are doing. It flatters man's ideas of his superiority over fish, and birds, and beasts. It encourages you to exercise in the open air, which means health. It fills you with satisfaction when you are successful: it never causes you to despair when you are not successful—"Hope springs eternal in the angler's breast." I do not know which of the charms is the greatest. Together they make a whole which promotes peace of mind and health of body. The one thing certain to me is that catching fish is not the chief charm of angling. The days when I have taken least have often appeared to me the best of days.' For my part, I find myself in entire accord with this. Some of the days that stand out most pleasantly, in regard not only to fishing but also to shooting, are those in which the bag has happened to be slight. When the angler's pannier is very heavy at the end of the day, it may mean that the fishing has been, if anything, over easy. The angler, as well as the gunner, has surely room to exult when, by the exercise of all his sporting wits, by clever stalking and other means, he has overcome after much difficulty a wary wild creature.

In Sir Edward Grey's delightful appreciation of angling I have found a title for this chapter. 'I suppose for most of us,' he writes, 'the earliest attraction of fishing has been the simple pleasure of excitement: in youth, at any rate, this has probably been so. There are certainly occasions of supreme excitement in fishing, such for instance as the moment when a salmon rises and is hooked, or the playing of an unexpectedly large trout, or sea-trout or grilse on a small rod and with light tackle. At such times excitement reaches a very high pitch, and is followed, if the fish is landed, especially when one is unaided and alone, by a state of happiness that cannot easily be described.

'We must, however, admit, whatever our peculiar preference may be, that this sort of pleasure belongs to other pursuits also, and I wish to dwell upon what seems to me a special charm of fishing rather than upon one which it shares with other sports.

'There is, in the first place—if we are thinking of trout-fishing—the charm of clean running water; the various moods and the life and movement of a stream come to fascinate an eye which has been used to watch them. In any view of country, water has a great attraction : there is a light upon it, which makes it seem itself to be the eye of the landscape ; we are drawn towards it, and we find near it the best trees and grass, or wealth of flowers and green things, and the greatest number of birds. To such places does fishing take us, and most often at the best time of the year. That seems to me the great charm of trout-fishing : it takes us to the most beautiful places in May and

June. These are the months when politics, the law, business, and professions of all kinds, society, all the duties that London can impose and all the pleasures it can offer, combine to deprive us of the country. At this time of year all these things are in a conspiracy against the season of the year and the happiness of some of us. Those who care for hunting or shooting will not help us, and of all the three great sports fishing alone is our friend. In May and June the trout are at their best: if we miss these months, we miss the best trout-fishing of the year.

'As we grow older we may hook fewer fish, and the moments of excitement, though still looked forward to, may come less often, and we may care more and more for the delights of the place and season. There is no noise nor hurry about our sport to disturb them, and the angler is independent, often alone, and free to enjoy them when and how he will. It is true that fly-fishing is hard work—there is none harder than dry-fly fishing when the trout are rising; but the

Our Friend Angling

trout seldom or never rise all day, and on most days, especially for dry-fly fishermen, there are hours of abundant leisure when the beauty of things around him may "sink down into his heart and hold him like a dream." And so in thinking of the charm of fishing there are thoughts of sky and running water and the songs of birds and bright air and long days, making in memory a typical picture of what has been and may be again.

'The records of the fishing of each of us will differ: some of us have not caught such large fish nor so many as others, though most of us have probably had certain triumphs and supreme moments, which we would not have exchanged for anything else that sport could offer. Of all these things we may have different tales to tell, but the great sense of pleasure is abundant, and may be common to all who have leisure and the will to fish.'

Anything which I could say on the question would but fall flat after such thoughtful words as these. I conclude, therefore, with an extract from one of Froude's essays: 'Neither the art of fly-fishing nor the enjoyment of it, when once acquired and tasted, will leave us except with life.'

CHAPTER II

A Stream and a Garden

It may be fancy, of course, for memory that gilds the past has a habit of playing these tricks; but I never can bring myself to believe that there is another so perfect a trout-stream as that which flowed by the old manor-house, a mile or so from the once important but, now that agriculture has depreciated, intensely sleepy and slow little town of N. in Berkshire. The manor-house stands not quite alone; a tiny hamlet clusters around it. There is still the blacksmith's forge, no doubt, with its splendid ruddiness by night; and still, no doubt, the village shop where you may buy your boots, your candles, your household utensils, your stationery—in fact, your everything. The quaint gabled vicarage is there too, the church with its fine Norman tower, and the churchyard with aged, half-sunken tombstones, which mark the dim resting-places of the once dear departed. The trout-stream flows through the hamlet, and boasts—or used to —a mill-wheel, a few yards from the gate of the manor-house. It was pleasant in the long summer days, in the sensuous June evenings, to lean restfully over the bridge and watch the motion of the dripping wheel, or go nearer and enjoy the aroma of the pearly white grain, which covered the walls, the floor of the mill, and the burly miller himself. Glancing up from the water, one could just see the top windows of the manor-house over the great brick wall. As viewed thus, the place looked the reverse of inviting. Even in the height of summer, you would scarcely have deemed it worthy a visit.

Once inside the gate, I found the house, outwardly at least, much as I had pictured it; plain to severity, and very Hanoverian.

A Stream and a Garden

Waiting at the door, however, I remarked with approval that the stream flowed close to the house, so close that you might hook a trout from one of the lower windows. The hall of the old place was of noble dimensions, with a broad, gently sloping staircase, of the kind peculiar to old country houses; and the chief reception-room one of great attractiveness, having fine bay windows and many quiet nooks and corners. The walls were decked with none of your modern fashionable papers, but hidden by old oak panelling, whilst the floor was also of oak, smooth and polished. One of the windows opened on to a lawn and a flower-garden, through the centre of which ran the trout-stream, spanned by several small bridges. There were

'. . . sinuous paths of lawn and moss,
Which led through the garden along and across;
Some open at once to the sun and the breeze,
Some lost among bowers of blossoming trees.'

There were, too, many beds and borderings of lovely flowers, such as the dahlia, geranium, verbena, calceolaria—brown and yellow speckled — sweet mignonette, and phloxes of a hundred hues—all in 'sweet disorder.' As for the walls of the manor-house, they were covered with creepers having gnarled stems like the greater branches of an aged oak. Somewhere on the walls was a sundial, half hidden be sure in due season by the purple passion-flowers. It is hard after these years to locate it exactly, but it was there, and the shadows crept regretfully over it.

The stream broke into music as it entered this garden, and low and sweetly among the thousand, thousand blooms sang its everlasting lullaby song. Where a great plane-tree swept the water with its lowest and heaviest bough, one looked with confidence in the summer evening for a few good rising trout. There was a deep hole under the roots of this tree, and out of this the fish would come when all was quiet—trout are great believers in quietude—and roam about under the branches, picking up a good meal of insects which fell out of the thick foliage

A Stream and a Garden

above. Though a rod was usually to be seen lying about the lawn, or upright against the walls of the old house, the trout were not much assailed, and therefore not hard to hook. An ideal stream it was, no doubt, for dry-fly and gossamer gut; but then, unfortunately, the fish, being scarcely half educated, would take it wet and on thick gut.

The worst of fishing in this charming stream was that the hostess would always send out to ask you to come in and have lunch, or tea, or dinner. At other times, just as one was reckoning for certain on hooking a two-pound trout, the girls of the house would stop on their way to the kitchen-garden after fruit, and then, of course, good-bye to the catching of fish. A wonderful place was this kitchen-garden; everything in it grew to such an exorbitant size. The scarlet-runners were so tall that you could scarcely touch their straggling tops with your walking-stick, and then there were the mightiest gourds and melons to be left for seed and harvest decorations. Flowers, too, there were along the prim box hedges; phloxes here again; wallflowers, lavender, great white lilies with yellow-dusted petals, lilies of the valley, fair to youth and pale to passion; larkspur; immense sunflowers. The girls would stop now and then, and pluck a bloom of becoming colour; one of them, who, like Maud in her splendour, might be called the fairest flower of all, has now, alas, no further need of earthly gardens.

No doubt the garden after all these years is in the flower time still bright with its blossoms, and under the great plane-tree where the stream flows deep and mysterious the trout will still be on the look-out for insect food, perhaps as little harassed as in old days. But were I to return thither, rod in hand, there would certainly be a great something lacking; the garden would be changed, as, perhaps, was that in which grew the sensitive plant, and the stream bound to disappoint, even if the trout rose freely.

A Stream and a Garden

When I angled there, it was the heyday of summer—summer of nature and of boyhood; now it is past mid-winter, and this perhaps would explain the sure deterioration in that Eden of colour and odour, and in that limpid trout-stream.

CHAPTER III

A Hertfordshire Trout

HE was at once the most careless and the craftiest of anglers. Careless, because he was wont to fish with a battered old rod, with a line that had been long since worn away at the tapering end, so that it no longer tapered, with flies that no self-respecting tacklemaker would for a moment own to. Crafty, because he would watch a moving trout for an hour, never casting to him till the right moment; would peer and pry into all manner of odd, out-of-the-way, and, to many folk, impossible nooks and corners in search of fish; would dib right through a thick alder bush, or over a low willow bough; would move along the banks, when on the look-out for prey, with all the stealthiness and the care that are

A Hertfordshire Trout

displayed by a poacher in the neighbourhood of the gamekeeper's cottage; would stalk a three-pounder as though it were a twelve-pointer. He was so careless of his personal appearance, so *simplex munditiis*, that some folk could scarcely believe that he was a sportsman at all, for there are those who seem to think that it is part of the whole duty of an angler to rig himself out in stereotyped sporting costume, and to stick his cap full of flies that are never used. Thus he often walked along the banks of his beloved south-country trout-stream—where the very willows and rushes must have known him—in precisely the same attire in which he walked along the streets of London. Any old clothes did for this careless-crafty angler, and he commonly wore a hard black-felt hat, very old and rusty about the rim owing to exposure to the weather. Report had it that he was once seen walking down New Bond Street, in the height of the London season, with sand-shoes; the aforementioned rusty old felt; coat, trousers, and waistcoat of different patterns;

holding a rod in one hand and several trout strung together with a bit of thick string in the other. This sounded unlikely, because he would scarcely have been in Bond Street at that hour of day during the fishing season.

Until you saw him at work stalking, casting to, or playing a trout, you might be led away into thinking that he was a very amateurish sportsman. Once see him, however, at work, and you could not fail to recognise a master mind and master hand. With small fish of barely 'limit' size, or only an ounce or inch or two above the 'limit,' he had no quarrel, and would often put such gently back; against weighty trout he waged a relentless war, carrying it right into their most fortified camps, even amongst the villainous roots of old waterside trees, and where snags were most thickly planted in the bed of the stream. The man knew no fear, and it was astonishing how rarely he got broken, even when fishing with a single small fly and fine gut.

One dark, uninviting afternoon in April,

A Hertfordshire Trout

when there was more of winter than of spring in the air, and when the edges of the stream, which would by and by be a jungle of greenery, white meadowsweet, and pink willow-herb blossoms, were still bare and exposed, our careless-seeming one came down with a friend from town for an hour or two to see, in his own language, 'if there was anything doing.' He bought a few alders on the way to the station, with a couple of casts; his fly-case was in his breast coat-pocket, and his rod, winch, and landing-net—an intensely plebeian net, that cost, perhaps, when new, about five shillings—were at the hut, which had not been entered since the end of last season. There was a certain back stream of about a hundred yards in length pertaining to the fishery, famous for good fish which rarely moved till the evening, even then seldom rising at anything save a green drake or spent gnat. As the evening drew in, with its leaden sky and chilly wind, the old angler and his companion came and pried into this back stream, and soon perceived the first moving fish they had come across that day. It was a trout on a shrimping expedition, breaking the surface of the water right in under the bank, against which the wind was blowing hard and clean across stream. To get at the fish from the side of the river where the anglers were situated looked a very difficult task. The old angler, nothing if not unselfish, gave the rod to his friend and bade him have a try, but the friend could not get the fly—a big alder, fished down stream with plenty of movement to deceive the shrimper—to travel to the right spot. To fish under one bank by the back-handed cast with a cruel wind against one is a grievous trial. The wind took the fly, the whole gut cast, indeed, right on to the bank time after time.

Meanwhile the trout was working up stream, always keeping under the bank. A few minutes more and, unless he turned and came down, he would be in deep water, where tailing fish could not be 'spotted.' The old angler, being appealed to, then took

A Hertfordshire Trout

the rod, and, by using his left hand, got to the fish in wonderful style the very first cast. The fish came with a big wave, and missed somehow, and then for the first time his two pursuers saw and knew for certain that he must be a heavy one. Three times he came, and the third time the rod bent gloriously into a bow, strained to its uttermost. What a fight, and what a strain on mind as well as on rod and tackle whilst it lasted! But the gallant fish was ladled out, his course being run; a five-pounder to the ounce, and the famous stream, though it may have yielded a few heavier fish in its time, has surely never yielded a more splendid specimen. It was only when the deed was done, the rod taken to pieces, and the gut examined in the now faint light, that a second fly was discovered on the cast, though the anglers believed they were fishing with one large fly, namely, the alder, which the trout took just under water. The second fly was a small blue upright, and, looking into the matter, the old angler exclaimed he knew how it was—he could not have used that cast since the preceding spring, when the two friends were angling for the troutlets of delicious Barle.

Was ever such carelessness! Nevertheless, the gut had held; and as for the fish, it was taken back to town wrapped up in newspaper, which the anglers had brought down to glance through in case there should be nothing doing all day. They had not troubled to bring a creel, as the chance of getting anything to put in it on such an uncharitable day seemed remote. It was by far the best fish of the season, though the old angler has since declared that one evening later on he saw and pursued a trout about the same spot, which made him look to and test his cast very carefully indeed. The back stream towards night is the very place for adventures.

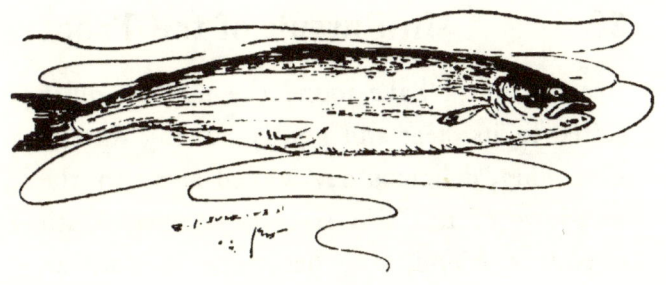

CHAPTER IV

The Little Pang

DRY-FLY fishing is a branch of the angler's art which has only been developed within the last quarter of a century. Neither Walton nor Cotton ever dreamt of such a thing in their philosophies, and even now the practice is not very commonly resorted to by trout fishermen save in the case of the clear-running streams of the south of England and one or two of the Derbyshire and Staffordshire waters.[1] On many of the chalk streams of the south it is essential to success. The Pang, which enters the Thames at Pangbourne, is not one of the regular dry-fly

---

[1] But Mr. Cheney, the head of the great piscicultural department of the United States, writes telling me he believes it will be resorted to in America.

streams, but I have found the method quite suited to its clear and gently flowing waters. One long, delicious day whiled away in the meadows of this tiny river in company with a college friend, who has since become an enthusiast and an expert in dry-fly work, will often slip into my thoughts when pondering over fishing days and ways in many waters.

It was a beautiful May morning, just before the time when the verdure of spring is lost in the uncalculated wealth of summer. From the old-fashioned village inn we crossed the road, and passed into the green water meadows, through which the bright water glided with an oily smoothness. Thrushes were singing their loudest; blackbirds fluted mellow notes from the topmost branch of oak and elm; the nightingale's song rang out from the hedgerows; butterflies, brimstone and orange tip, came out in the early morning sunshine, and tortoiseshells too after their long winter sleep. All living things in the fields and woods were

The Little Pang

full of movement, of ecstasy in the awakened spring. Following the windings of the stream, we came to a rustic wooden bridge, and leaning over noted the first moving trout. He was occasionally sucking-in an olive dun. Getting behind the fish and on the opposite bank, I sent across to him a fine imitation of the natural fly which was coming on in small quantities. He rose instantly, but missed; and after this nothing would induce him to look at either natural or artificial again. Turning our steps again up stream after this slight repulse, we were suddenly startled by a great splashing and shouting, an unwelcome and very unexpected warning of an otter-hunt at hand, and in a few minutes, sure enough, by us they came, a motley crew of dogs and men of high and low degree—chiefly, it seemed, the latter. The hunt soon swept past, being bound for a point several miles up stream, where, it was rumoured in the neighbourhood, an otter, or at least the remains of an otter feast, had been lately seen. All hope of sport for an hour or more to come in the main stream in which hounds and men had been wildly splashing was rudely dispelled; so we walked up to some little tributaries about a mile distant. It was an easy jump across the widest of these streams, yet all were well stocked with nice fish up to a pound and a-half and sometimes even two pounds in weight. Midday still found us with an almost empty creel, for the rise was slight. Espying a farmhouse across the meadows, we went up and begged a glass of milk, as the sun was hot.

After quenching our thirst we turned towards the stream again. A rivulet flowed right through the farmyard, forming a pond, which was clear and shallow. Imagine trout-fishing in a farmyard! We took a fish here, and several more just beyond the house, where the water was overhung with brambles and rather rapid in parts. The rise of fly was soon over, so we gave up fishing for a while and explored the course of the little brook. It is quite an ideal trout-stream. Even though fish cannot be caught just now while

The Little Pang

we are waiting for a fresh hatch of fly to take place, surely all around there is that which should fill the mind with content. True, it is too early for the June wild-roses, with their white petals, which 'go straight to the heart'; nor is the fragrant meadow-sweet in bloom yet a while; but cowslips and marsh marigold are gorgeous in the meadows, and the wheat never looks more beautiful than in this its vigorous youth.

In the copse hard by is a dell dyed blue by hyacinth: wood-anemones are there too, and slender cuckoo-flowers. A kingfisher flashes by in the sunlight, and at our approach a moor-hen dives out of sight with a great spluttering. Wagtails of two species are running about, never very far from the cattle, and the breasts of some of these birds are yellow as the marigold itself. At the thin, feathery edge of the copse, and within a few paces of the water, there is a wild-duck's nest. In some rank herbage overhanging the water a dabchick is sitting on two stained eggs; seeing us, she slips into the stream; and when we return, half an hour later, the eggs appear to have been taken away; but the bird has merely covered them over with a few dead leaves. You have only to sit quite still for a while, and the dabchick and wild-duck will both return to their nests. The water-rat fearlessly swims about within a few yards of you, while a rustling in the copse announces the approach of a timorous leveret. As for the sedge-warbler, he will come into the bush under which you are reclining and pour that quaint medley of notes—stolen notes, say some—into your very ears. But make the slightest movement and he instantly leaves off singing,[1] whilst the leveret rushes off in terror, and the dabchick slips into the water again. As for the fish, a shadow will alarm them; indeed, you must stalk your trout just as you stalk on summer evenings a rabbit feeding in the woodland path or a deer on the

---

[1] On the other hand, fling a stone in the bush where the sedge-warbler lurks silent, and he will instantly burst into song.

The Little Pang

hillside. Practice and care alone will tell the angler how near he can approach a fish without alarming it. And herein, to no small extent, lies the difference between a good and a bad fly-fisherman. The former creeps patiently towards his fish inch by inch, and often on hands and knees; he makes one or two casts in the air, to judge the distance to a nicety, and keeps the point of his rod well down, to avoid flinging a shadow on the water. The latter strides forward with his rod held straight up, and instantly makes a bungling cast. The trout sees the rod or the angler himself, and is gone like a flash of lightning.

Fly-fishing in our chalk streams is indeed a distinct branch of the art of angling. It takes us through no wild mountainous scenery like that of the North, but through peaceful fields and woodlands, and by clear limpid streams, where there is the fragrance of the flowers, the brimful joy of the summer days, and the ever-murmurous refrain of the brook.

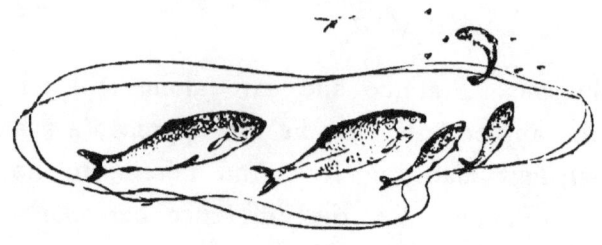

CHAPTER V

The Angling Excuse

A CYNIC has remarked that there is something in the misfortunes of our friends not altogether distasteful to us; I shall not deny, for my part, that I have known a feeling the reverse of disagreeable when that no doubt very well-meaning fellow, but all the same intensely self-confident angler, Swellcast, has returned to our angling inn with an absolutely empty creel. There are some men you never feel the least resentment towards, though day after day they return with heavy creel, while you yourself cannot get hold of a single sizable fish, flog you every inch of water never so long and so carefully. Who can, for instance, begrudge the truly modest angler his good luck, when he is always ready

The Angling Excuse

to explain that he happened by the merest chance to fall in with a number of rising trout at a particularly cosy corner in the stream; and that, also by the merest chance in the world, he was so fortunate as to hook every one of them securely? As a matter of fact, you know perfectly well that he filled his creel with trout because he angled uncommonly well, and that you failed to fill yours, or a quarter fill it, because you bungled with fish after fish, and wasted the best part of the day hammering away at a rise which eventually turned out to be that of a disgusting little six-inch grayling or even a dace. It makes no difference; you cannot nourish the least feeling of hostility towards him. But with the arrogant angler who never makes a bag without making a bawl about it, who will have it that the trout were rising rather badly than well in the particular stretch he was fishing, and that, if he had been elsewhere, he would have filled his creel thrice over, it is altogether different. When this sort of angler has a thoroughly bad day while all the other rods on the water have done something, his misfortunes will be more than tolerable to you, even though you regard him, apart from fishing, as a good fellow and even a friend. The worst of it is, when he is without trout he is rarely, if ever, without an excuse or two. You see him returning home, as you stand on the steps outside the angling inn chatting with two or three friends in regard to the day's sport and the prospect of the morrow, and know—intuitively from his dejected manner, which he vainly tries to hide—that he has had a simply shocking time of it. 'Well, have you got 'em all?' is the well-worn witticism which one of the party tries on him by way of accentuating and bringing home to him his misfortune. 'Oh, I only turned out about an hour ago to see if there was an evening rise,' is the reply; 'have scarcely cast a fly all day.' If he has got only one trout, he will very likely say he killed that in the morning, and that then, seeing there was not much doing, he turned in,

The Angling Excuse

wrote letters, and had lunch. He will never honestly confess that he has been fishing hard all day, being mad to get a dish of trout and crow over all the other anglers on the water; though you may know perfectly well that such has been his little game.

Different anglers cultivate different kinds of excuses. One, for instance, almost invariably tells you that he turned in early in the afternoon and had a long sleep; while another broke the top of his rod just as the rise of the day was commencing, and, having no twine, was unable to mend it in time to fill his creel, which, of course, he could have done with ease had it not been for this curious bit of bad luck. A very common excuse is that there was absolutely no fly and no fish moving all day long on the particular stretch of water on which the troutless angler was fishing; sometimes, however, this excuse is made in perfect sincerity by anglers who are not ashamed of, but merely puzzled by, their want of success.

Who has not met the angler that never seems to perceive fly sailing down stream, unless it be hatching in thousands, and rarely notes a trout rising unless it be creating a splash in the operation? He constantly goes up to every rod on the water to inquire, 'What are they taking?'—a very aggravating type of angler this, who, one feels sure, will never go far in the art of fly-fishing.

One of the keenest men on killing trout you can recollect meeting at an angling inn attempts to make out that he has not primarily come down to angle, but to get a little fresh air and change of scene; and when you ask him about his day's sport he usually suggests something to that effect, which is his idea of the most dignified way of excusing his ill-success. When he does happen to get hold of a brace of trout—which is, to tell the truth, a somewhat unusual occurrence out of may-fly season—he contrives to let everybody in the inn know of it, while pretending that it is utterly immaterial to him whether

The Angling Excuse

his creel be empty or no. Everybody who has known him for a week knows of this pretence, and he, being a fairly shrewd man, is probably quite well aware that his excuses and devices deceive nobody; yet, curiously enough, he persists in them, and probably will till the end—so strong is the force of habit. To the excuses of the bumptious angler like the aforementioned Swellcast, few will be prepared to lend an indulgent ear, seeing that the man, when not in need of them, will always be crowing, either directly or indirectly, over those who have fared ill at the river-side. But the ordinary angling excuses—such as no fly, vile wind, bad stretch of water, too many anglers out, indifferent artificial flies, 'short-rising,' no fish in the stream, glaring sunshine, etc., put forward in good faith by the unfortunate—these it were well perhaps not to treat too scornfully, since one never can tell when one may not be in want of several of them oneself in order to explain away an exceedingly bad day or week. It has sometimes seemed to me that if trout only knew the anxiety and humiliation human beings were put to in order to explain the reasons for empty creels, they would feel fully avenged of their occasional capture by rod and line.

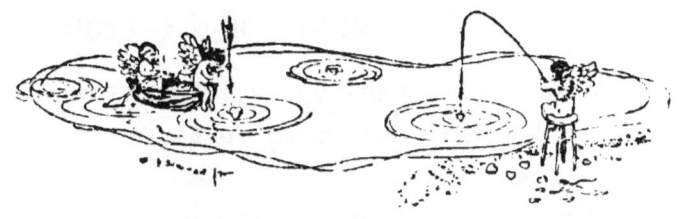

CHAPTER VI

In Taddington Dale

THE River Wye—the Derbyshire Wye—is one that grows upon the angler and the lover of nature. The more he sees of it the more he warms towards it. It is the most devious of streams, threading its way from Bakewell, and far above, to Haddon, Filiford, and Rowsley, where it mingles with the peat-brown waters of the Derwent—threading its fastidious way through rugged valley and through meadow-land in a long succession of curves and sharp turns. These curves make many deep and sluggish back-waters, into which the surface food is driven and in which confined till it finds its way down the mouths of the lusty trout that affect such spots. It is pleasant to sit down on the protruding root of an old willow, with heavy-foliaged boughs that gently touch, in summer time, the face of the stream; to rest motionless, and listen to the sound of the water rippling, here most gently, almost imperceptibly, but breaking into loud chorus a hundred yards or so further down, as it forces its way over a bed of shingle. Thus reclining, you may presently attune yourself to nature, provided the fish are not stirring. If they are, and you be an angler, the instinct of sport must predominate, and the one supreme question be how best to present your lure.

A day on a choice stretch of the Wye above Ashford, and amongst the most beautiful and wooded of the Derbyshire dales, is an invitation not to be lightly refused by the angler, or the man to whom fine scenery is a perpetual feast. So when such an invitation was one spring day made to me, I accepted it with delight. We, my host and I, started one bright May morning, taking in the dogcart with us a well-tried cane

In Taddington Dale

rod and an assortment of fly-books and angling tackle sufficient to catch and carry away half the fish in the stream. From Bakewell to Taddington Dale is a delightful drive on a fine spring morning. The river is scarcely ever out of both sight and sound, and between Ashford—a pleasantly situated little place—and Taddington village there is some rugged mountain scenery, to see the equal of which English people would think nothing of travelling to Switzerland, or of crossing the North Sea to the Land of the Midnight Sun. In Taddington Dale the scenery of this part of Derbyshire is perhaps at its finest. Even in the early and not too leafy days of May it is beautiful. Think, then, what these delicious dales must be like in the gorgeous midsummer, or later in the year when autumn lays 'a fiery finger on the leaf' and rides through these lonely places of the earth with the west wind as her chariot!

We drove slowly by the river-side in Taddington Dale, my companion pointing out with pride the fine pools and the 'flats' where the trout lay waiting for the rise of fly. The sun came sparkling through the budding sycamores, and flashed on the tender greening things by the wayside. The finches were full of life and movement, singing as though there were no such season in bird life as winter; whilst the charming small willow-wren, running through its low sweet song, told that the summer must be near, though one could still see through the ash-trees. In Taddington Dale we drew up, and my companion pointed out a little wooden shed, where he stabled his horse when on a fishing expedition in the neighbourhood. The river was within a few yards of the hut, and in a few minutes we were on the water with one rod between us, and with a creel which we feared would not be big enough for the morning's sport. Alas! the creel proved even less serviceable than we thought, though from a different cause. The result of an hour or so on the water was absolutely futile so far as sport

In Taddington Dale 47

went. A furious north wind sprang up as we reached the water-side. Dry-fly fishing became quite impossible. Presently it blew a small gale, ruffling the water to such an extent that we could not spy a rising fish. The line and hook went everywhere save into the mouths of the trout. At length we found two fish well 'up' in a fairly sheltered pool, and I set to work to put the fly—a prettily dressed olive—over one of them. Just as I was hoping to drop the fly like the proverbial piece of thistle-down on the water, there came a vicious little gust that whirled the line into a cruel-looking hawthorn which overhung the pool. My companion at once volunteered to go aloft. I gathered that he had been in the bush before, and knew the worst thorns. Up he went, uttering curious little sounds of distress when an unusually stubborn prickle buried itself in his flesh. At length he got hold of the fly, and commenced the process of disentanglement. As fast as the line was freed from one branch it coiled itself round another. When at last the line was really free, both fish had ceased rising ; and as the wind had by this time increased to the proportions of a hurricane, we decided to put up the rod and get back to the hut to lunch. It went against the grain to leave the water, but as fishing under such circumstances was quite out of the question, we decided, after lunch, to make a little pilgrimage to Demons Dale, which lay hard by.

Demons Dale is not unknown to North of England anglers and tourists, though it has not the fame of some of the larger dales—such as Monsal—near at hand. So wonderful a bit of scenery, in so small a compass, is scarcely to be seen in the narrowest and deepest of the Norwegian fjords. The Dale is entered from below by a dark footpath through a clump of firs, and though within a short distance of the highroad, no glimpse of it can be obtained till the entrance, or mouth, is reached. It appears to be, and possibly is, nothing more nor less than a large crack, or fissure, in the hillside.

In Taddington Dale

It is exceedingly narrow; the giants of the fairy tales would be able to take it nicely at one stride, without stretching their legs overmuch, and unfortunately—if that word can be applied to anything in nature—it is also very short. A few minutes after entering Demons Dale, from below, you find yourself at the top, and in a beaten footpath again amongst the open hills. The walls of the Dale run sheer up on both sides at its lowest and deepest end; so steep, indeed, are they that even the plants and ferns which usually flourish in such spots can scarcely find roothold. Entering this weird place, we scared several jackdaws nesting over the shelves of rock; they rose and winged themselves away without a protest, silent as their haunt. The silence of the place was indeed quite oppressive. We were tempted to break it for a few moments. To dislodge from above a huge boulder, roll it to the edge, and push it over was accomplished almost as soon as thought of. It passed into space with a rushing sound, fell upon a shelf, which it dinted and battered; then one more frantic leap, and it thundered on to a rock harder than itself, and burst into innumerable fragments.

As we found Demons Dale so we left it, slumbering. Lingeringly we retraced our footsteps to the outer world, driving home to Bakewell by Ashford, and through noble Chatsworth Park; our creel was empty, but we did not think that we had gone forth to angle quite in vain.

CHAPTER VII

A Seven-Pounder

THE place of all places for very heavy trout, for great lusty fellows which may be relied upon when hooked to make the reel sing a merry tune to commence with, and to make the exasperated angler curse the maker of his gut-casts to end with, is a sedately flowing, clear brook in the land of chalk streams, where weed-cutting is rarely resorted to, and where no artificially reared trout are ever put into the water. A quarter of a century or so since a friend made the glorious discovery, in one of the home counties, of a stretch of trouting water which he saw might be turned into an admirable fly-fishing club for a dozen rods. He got a lease of it at a very moderate figure, and set to work to put it in order. It was almost choked up with weeds, and overgrown in many parts with miscellaneous underwood and thorn-bushes. The trout were few, but they were nearly all giants. It was necessary to get these fellows out of the brook before any yearlings or fry were put in. My friend, with the aid of another willing angler, set to work and took from the water the majority of the fish, which he is prepared to swear averaged upwards of four pounds apiece. Imagine the sport these fish must have given in a brook so neglected as this one had been for a matter of years! Fit for a king it must have been; and, from his glowing accounts, actually was.

Not so many miles from that spot as the crow flies is a stretch of water which the same inveterate angler—who has probably killed, during his long fishing career, as many heavy trout as any man living—has also, on more than one occasion, described to me in terms of the highest praise. Once, in the Eighties, he went thither with a boon com-

A Seven-Pounder

panion. It was a day of days, and the trout were landed so fast that at length the two anglers took counsel. Said one, 'Look here, we must stop this; I get a pound fish at almost every cast.' Replied the other, 'So do I. Let us return everything under two pounds.' Before long it was necessary to hold a second council, the situation being more serious than ever. 'I say, old fellow,' exclaimed one of the distressed anglers, 'the two-pounders are coming out dreadfully thick now.' So the limit was further raised to two and a-half pounds. Even then there was considerable slaughter, and the carnage before the end of the day's sport was quite appalling. The owner, however (who hated fishing himself, and deemed it very slow work indeed), was not in the least disturbed, and encouraged his diffident guests to fish on, if so they chose, to the troutful end.

Towards the close of may-fly season—to be precise, on Whit Monday, 1895—it fell to my lot to fish the stretch of water immediately below the spot where the two-pounders came out so very often on that occasion. The water was in a woful state of neglect. Enormous bunches of weeds asserted themselves in both pool and stream, and here and there—especially when a mill above held up the water—seemed to well-nigh choke up the brook. Now and again, strolling along the banks, I caught sight of a great wave and a shadowy form in precipitate flight. A few spent may-flies, with some duns and spinners, were out in the bright sunshine, but the fish never stirred. The only movement of a feeding trout was occasionally that of a great tail, which, breaking the surface of the pellucid stream, showed that water-shrimp and snail must be abundant enough in the weed-beds. Later on in the evening there were a few dimples, and presently I caught sight of a fish in a streamy place and close to the surface. The size of a fish, in a place of this description, is often most deceptive; now a half-pounder looks a good pound and a-half, and now a three-pounder scarcely more than a third of its actual weight.

A Seven-Pounder

This fish seemed to be about a pound. He rose at the second or third cast, and took the fly with perfect confidence. A short rush up stream, a quick return, and he was well in the weeds. The line almost immediately slacked in that sickening manner all anglers know so well. This trout must have been, at the least, a two-pounder. In a little bay or backwater twenty yards higher up stream I came, a few minutes after this mishap, upon a great trout lying close to the surface, and obviously on the look-out for prey. I instantly stepped back, and then, on hands and knees, peered over the bank with the uneasy feeling that I should find I had scared him. He was still in position, however, and the may-fly was cast to him without delay. There was a slight drag, but before the stream had had time to take the 'cockiness' out of the fly, the great fellow came up and drew it swiftly in. When these very heavy trout are really feeding at the surface there is no nonsense about them. I gave him perhaps a couple of seconds' grace, and then struck hard. He went below, and bored about there like a salmon for a quarter of a minute or so. Then, feeling the killing strain of the rod bent double—for out of weeds he had to be kept at all hazards—up stream he tore, taking out the line in splendid style. A second pause, and down he came, like the smaller fish just hooked and lost, only right under my feet. Of all trout manœuvres, and they are neither few nor far between, this is probably the most effective, as it nearly always results in slack line, or, at any rate, in a considerable lessening of the rod's strain on the fish. Once under my feet, he plunged into a huge bed of weeds, and there was an end of it. I tried all the devices to entice him out, but in vain, and, in the end, when the line was freed, it was minus the fly and a small portion of the cast. The trout, not of a day, nor of a season, but of a lifetime, had thus dreadfully gone!

What *was* the weight of this trout? I asked myself again and again on my sad way home; and, look at the matter how I would,

A Seven-Pounder

I felt it was impossible to conscientiously put him down at under five pounds; indeed, it more than once occurred to me that it was false modesty to set him down at an ounce under seven pounds, and on at least one occasion during day-dreams he has pulled down the scale at something decidedly heavier than even the latter weight. Later that same evening—which was one of the most oppressively warm I have ever known by the river-side—I took a beautiful trout of well over three pounds, and that made some slight amends for the dire disaster with the possible seven-pounder, or, to put it in another way, for the five-pounder-at-the-very-least. Most anglers have a fish of this character to dwell upon at suitable seasons—a fish which has become 'a memory and a pang.'

CHAPTER VIII

The Upright Angler

HE wore spectacles, which he would, when his attention was directed to anything that was going on in the water, carefully take off, examine, wipe with his pocket-handkerchief, and replace on his nose. When the settled conviction took possession of him that there was a feeding trout at a certain exposed spot in the stream, he would proceed to stalk it in a manner peculiar to his type. First of all he stood bolt upright, and then, lest that should prove ineffectual in apprising the fish of his presence, he made quite a point of holding his rod straight up over his shoulder. Instead of creeping, in the miserable manner in which some of his bankside companions were wont to do, towards

The Upright Angler

his fish, or towards the place where his fish had been feeding when he first observed it, and putting himself in humiliating postures, such as are effected by mere dry-fly purists and others, he walked upright to the edge of the stream. Then, and not till then, he was wont to examine his line and his flies and carefully disentangle them from any knots into which they might have tied themselves; because, as every one knows, fishing lines and flies have a habit of getting horribly mixed up just about the time when a good trout is seen rising.

These necessary preliminaries having been fulfilled, our angler would indulge in a few swishes, and end up by securely hooking the opposite bank. It was irritating, no doubt, but perhaps did not really make a very great difference, seeing that the trout had by that time in the vast majority of cases ceased feeding for some reason or other. Indeed, it may not have been a trout at all, but a water-hen or a rat which caused the splash that attracted this angler's attention. How is a fellow always to tell what it is that has made the disturbance in the waters when he has not seen it?

Sometimes he would not hook anything at all, not even the bank nor his own coat, nor the seat of a friend's breeks, in which case, being a thoughtful and intelligent man, with entomological leanings, he would come to the conclusion that he had not got hold of the right kind of fly for that particular day and weather. Two courses lay open to him, the first being to catch one of the insects flying about in the air, and the second to seek for information amongst the various other anglers who were engaged in fishing the stream within reasonable reach. He commonly resorted to the second expedient if there were any anglers nigh to question, and the words, 'What fly are they taking?' used to be fearfully familiar to those among his friends who did not give him a wide berth out fishing.

There was certainly no aloofness about the man, for, with the most perfect frankness and good-nature, he would constantly come

The Upright Angler

right up to any angler he might espy, no matter how slight the acquaintance, and inquire, 'What sport?' He must have often been puzzled, if not downright nettled, at the strange and chilling replies he received from anglers kneeling in the grass, regardless of wet knees, or lying almost flat down, and casting to a fish from that ridiculous position. Anglers whom he thus cheerfully accosted and joined would in some instances actually get up and stalk angrily away, without uttering a single word, or, at any rate, only one word, and that a very short, sharp one. Possibly he regarded such conduct as pure eccentricity, only to be looked for in anglers who could not fish standing up like men, but must needs crawl about on their bellies, like the lowest of the brute creation.

He was quite without prejudices and affectations in regard to the size of the fish he took. When he got a trout or a grayling out of the water he put it into his creel. Some foolish fellows were fond of talking about a limit and so forth, but he never troubled his head about matters of this kind. To put a fish back in the water because it happened to be under a pound or under ten inches he would, no doubt, have regarded as a bit of bumptiousness and 'side.' He kept them all; and yet the watchful water-keeper might have searched his creel and his person five days out of six without finding a single undersized fish. The keeper seemed, somehow, to be aware of this, and never thought of troubling our friend to show the inside of his fishing-creel.

He could fish by the book as well as most men, and was full of ingenious theories in respect especially to the best way of improving a fishery. His favourite proposition was that the first thing to do with your water was to put on a minnow and clean out the big trout from the deep pools; this he laid down again and again in the dining- and the smoking-room of every angling inn he entered. Thus somebody eventually named him the Minnow Man. A better name would have been, perhaps, the Upright Angler.

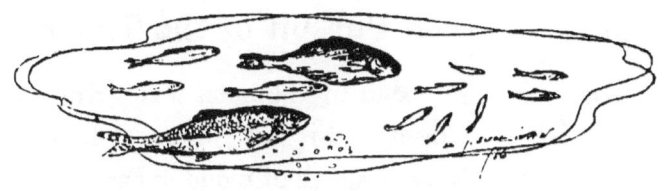

CHAPTER IX

Dibbing with the Dry-fly

DIBBING, or daping, with the artificial fly for big trout is a method of angling generally neglected, if not scorned, by many expert dry-fly fishermen. Yet it is a perfectly legitimate form of sport, often proving very killing when one might as well fish the highroad as the open stream. Moreover, it is one of the most scientific methods of using the dry-fly, necessitating, as it does, infinite patience, the most skilful stalking, and sometimes great coolness in playing a heavy fish in an awkward spot. I have a certain dry-fly stream in my mind's eye at the present time, in which dibbing has frequently enabled me to bring to creel plump and well-conditioned trout on days when scarcely a faint dimple has been observable in the open water from sunrise to sunset. In hot summer days, when there is not a speck of cloud in the sky, and when the garish sunlight pervades the stream, fishing in the ordinary way is usually quite profitless. Grayling, it is true, may frequently be taken at such times, but what dry-fly fisherman who is after trout will care to work through the heat and burden of the day for *Salmo thymallus*? It is just at these hopeless times that big trout may frequently be found feeding under the trees and amid the bushes. Indeed, my experience is that fish which haunt such spots are on the rise more or less all day, morning, noon, and evening. One of the chief attractions of dry-fly fishing is the fact that the angler is in so many cases able to see the whole performance, and to note in detail the habits and movements of the trout. In dibbing, or in casting in wooded places with a very short line, the angler sees with great clearness, as a rule, the fish he is stalking. Sometimes he is within a yard of his prey, suffering a zephyr breeze

Dibbing with the Dry-fly

to gently carry the well-dried fly over the tips of a bunch of willow-herbs or a big dock-leaf and lay it on the water a foot in front of the unsuspicious fish. The interest and excitement always seem to me to be greater in proportion as one is nearer the fish. The knowledge that the slightest false or clumsy movement cannot fail to scare the stalked fish is sport in itself. Another special attraction of dibbing is the constant belief that something very big indeed must be lurking amongst the bushes and the wooded margins of the stream. The trout that frequent such places are rarely of the sprat size. In the open stream, and even in backwaters and deep pools, you may waste hours upon hours over a gently dimpling fish, which you take to be monster, but eventually find to be—in size—a minnow. Perhaps the greatest charm, however, in groping about amongst the trees and bushes lies in the absolute seclusion and quietness of these nooks. No blundering brother-angler will come thither and spoil your sport; no unwelcome tourist rudely interrupt your communings with Nature. The sedge-warbler is good company, though he may for a while sing at you suspiciously from the river-side thickets. You may sink down now and then on some tangled island and watch for rises under the gnarled willows and great dock-leaves. It does not matter if you wait an hour without seeing the faintest ring on the water. You are attuning your heart and brain to the glorious harmony of summer. The fardels of life will drop from you, and be swept away on the stream. These are the hours in our lives—alas that they are so few!—which no good man dare call wasted.

I cannot to this day recall without emotion a struggle I had with a big trout in one of the most romantic spots of the Derbyshire Wye. On a still evening, when there is nothing to speak of moving in the open stream, I occasionally repair to a certain island, on which one may land when the water is low by means of some rough and rather rickety stepping-stones. This island is densely wooded, and in summer-time it has, by way

Dibbing with the Dry-fly

of undergrowth, beds of gigantic docks, nettles, and various water-loving plants. To press through this mass is quite a business, seeing that many of the plants grow six feet and even seven feet high. But a careful study of the place has enabled me to easily find my way to all the backwaters and eddies which abound on one side of the island. Once in may-fly season, when the drake was on in countless thousands and was being utterly rejected by the trout, I hooked and lost three fish in the space of half an hour dibbing from this island. A fifth fish, the smallest of the lot, I killed with my last olive dun. There is one backwater off the island which formerly was fishable from the mainland; but an alder-tree has fallen into the pool, and rendered casting with short or long line quite impossible. The pool is deep and sluggish, retaining for a long while, when the river is low, all surface food washed thither out of the strong current. At midsummer I left an olive in a beautiful trout of about one pound or one pound and a quarter, and I had long entertained a suspicion that there must be a very monster lurking somewhere in this hole.

One still evening this suspicion grew so strong and masterful that I left a rising fish to come down and land on the island. I crept through the docks, and peered cautiously into the sullen pool. A grand trout was swimming round and round the backwater, sucking in olives with a loud smacking sound. For a few seconds my heart seemed to have stopped beating. I would not have raised a finger or made a false movement for a five-pound note. When sufficiently recovered from this sudden shock, I sank down gently in the herbage—faded away, in fact, from the water's edge as a crafty old pike fades from sight among the weeds. Then I listened to learn whether or no I had scared the trout. No; the smacking sound still continued. I instantly cut down the gut cast to about eighteen inches in length, and attached thereto a new light olive dun. Then, on hands and knees, I once more approached the

Dibbing with the Dry-fly

water, and, after much manœuvring, gently pushed my rod through the branches of the fallen tree and dangled the fly over the trout, or rather over the spot which I calculated he would reach in a few moments in his circling course. When he was within a foot of my fly I dibbed it enticingly on the water. He took no notice whatever. My spirits fell a little. I would then have taken a five-pound note to make a false movement. Again and again I tried the same process, till the fly was quite sodden. Then the rod had to be gently withdrawn and the fly dried. Suddenly a smaller trout, about one pound in weight, came on to the scene, and at once sidled up to my fly. I rudely withdrew it from the water, annoyed by the intruder who threatened to spoil my anticipated sport. Equally indignant, the big trout suddenly made a vicious dart at the new-comer and butted him savagely on the side. Exit pounder amid commotion. Back sailed the victor, and at once recommenced sucking down the olives. To tell in detail how I had again and again to draw back the rod and dry the fly would fill a chapter. At length the monster came up to my fly and seized it with the innocence of a six-inch samlet. Before striking, I let him turn round and resume his course—a risky experiment perhaps, but I had tried the same thing before with success. Then I drove the hook home with a will, and instantly felt that I was well into the fish.

For a while he swam round and round the pool out of sight, as a salmon will sometimes do when first hooked. I had some loose line in my hand—an absolutely necessary precaution in dibbing—and paid it out grudgingly, knowing the terrible nature of the place. My rod was all but immovable, owing to a big branch which had fallen across my side of the backwater, and which must, I saw too well, prevent my steering the fish out into the open stream. Before a minute had slipped by, things began to be rather lively. He took several fierce rushes, in one instance carrying the point of my rod well under water, and keeping it there for half a minute,

Dibbing with the Dry-fly

for I dared not give him more line. I kept out of sight, and put as much strain on the line as I deemed possible without a breakage. The cast, though fine, was strong, and the fly well tested both as to hook and gut. Yet, with even these points in my favour, I felt with a cruel pang that I had met my master. The light was fast waning, and it would soon be impossible to see the line amidst the leaves and the snags. For fully five minutes after one of his fiercest rushes the fish swam round and round the backwater. I began to entertain hopes. But suddenly he changed tactics without a moment's notice, dashing right out of the pool into the open stream with irresistible strength. My line became entangled, as did the top of my rod, in the fallen branch, and the fight was over. Then a darkness came upon my spirit, deeper than the gloom which night with lavish hand was dealing out to Nature. One despairing glance at the scene of that stern struggle, and I gathered up landing-net and bag and hastily departed. It was one of those experiences which embitter most anglers' lives from time to time. These things do not happen every season, because such monsters are rarely to be found taking duns, or indeed any other fly, except an occasional juicy drake, but perhaps once a decade. Yes, those are cruel moments that follow the loss of a large trout after a long and fierce struggle.

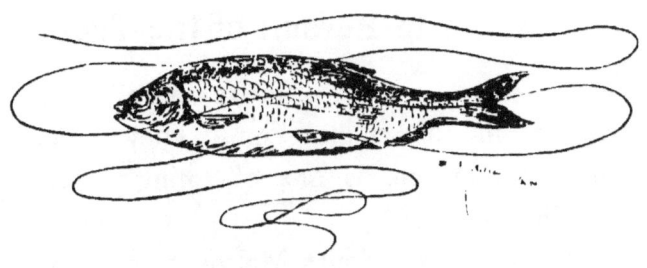

CHAPTER X

Wild Exmoor

It is sweet at times, when the heart is fretted and wearied by the strain and stress of town-life, to seek solace for even a few fleeting days with Nature in her rugged beauty.

Moved by the burning desire to quit for a brief while the whirl and glare of the city, I went down in the spring to wander on Exmoor. It was April, and the woods and hedges were growing tenderly verdant. The cuckoo's note was not yet heard; while the nightingale, for some mysterious reason, never goes so far west. But thrushes and blackbirds were singing as they never seem to sing later on; and a host of small birds swelled the chorus, amongst them the willow-wren, whose plaintive note every dweller in the country must know: he, like the cuckoo, is one of spring's chief harbingers.

The drive from South Molton to Simonsbath is very beautiful. For the first two or three miles, the road winds through a hilly and thickly wooded country—a typical Devonshire road, in fact. A sweet little stream brawls noisily along, generally close to the road, while some rich undulating water-meadows delight the eye. Presently we pass by a disused copper-mine, and through a quiet hamlet nestling on the confines of the moor itself. The meadows and birch-woods gradually melt away; and, climbing a steep long hill, we breathe a different air, that makes the pulse beat stronger, and the blood circle more freely in the veins. The Moor proper, in its wild desolation and its absolute silence, now opens out before us. Glancing back, we get a magnificent view of South Molton and its neighbourhood, even to hamlets and villages far remote. But the

Wild Exmoor

mists of night draw on apace, and we have yet to drive some half-dozen stiff miles before reaching that snug inn at Simonsbath, the 'William Rufus.' The snow still lies thick here and there along the roadside, in huge discoloured patches, grimly suggestive of the severity of the past winter. By and by a sudden turn of the road brings us in view of the 'Silver Barle.' At this turn, by the way, there is a grim precipice, with neither wall nor protection of any kind. To be hurled down that gully would seem certain death; and yet our driver tells how on a dark night, some years ago, a carriage and pair did actually go over, and with no graver casualty to the occupants than a broken collar-bone. The trap, however, was dashed to pieces, and it was a difficult business to extract the terrified horses.

The sound and sight of devious Barle send a thrill of joy through us, for we have come to fish in this stream, which abounds in trout, more, perhaps, than any of the other moorland streams; though they run very small—six or eight to the pound. Here and there, a monster of half a pound, or even three-quarters, may be taken with worm or fly.

Simonsbath is a little settlement in the midst of the wilds of Exmoor forest. I am referring to Exmoor proper, and not to the district commonly known by this name, which is of wide extent. This place, with its green plantations and few slight buildings, is an oasis in a wild but beautiful tract; nor do its simple and scanty signs of civilisation harmonise ill with the desolation around. A church, with a few labourers' cottages, an inn, and picturesque old mansion-house; add to these the fir plantations, that afford a shelter from the winter storms, and you have the civilisation of Exmoor complete. More than one attempt has been made to reclaim the forest. Many years ago, a mansion-house on a far more pretentious scale was commenced, but never completed; there it stands to this day, grim and untenanted save by the starlings, which build there in the spring. Other attempted improvements have failed in the same way : the peat and heather seem to defy the hand of man; and his little efforts to rob hill and dale of their natural grandeur and obdurate ruggedness are quite futile.

Early in the cold bright morning we were up to fish the Barle as far down as Landacre Bridge, or perhaps to wooded Withypoole. These upper reaches of the stream between Landacre and Simonsbath are undeniably a little monotonous; one continuous brawl over rocks and stones, with none of those deep, mysterious pools so delightful to the angler's heart; nor are there any swift, smooth 'runs.' At Withypoole, indeed, the Barle alters considerably in aspect, presenting a wide variety of river scenery : deep pools, 'stickles,' and quiet 'runs.' Yet, even at and above Simonsbath, the Barle to my mind is a lovely stream.

It is shining and snowing by fits, and consequently sport is very moderate; but here and there, during the short snow-storms, we pick up a few beautiful troutlets, that rise fearlessly to the fly, a march brown or blue upright. My companions stride on far ahead, leaving me a mile or so of river to fish. But the rise is very slight; for there is no sign as yet of the natural fly on the water, nor is the wind in the right quarter. Nevertheless, left to myself, I find plenty of solace. Passing an old disused copper-mine—there are many hereabouts—I find the place straightway a mine of memories. A solitary shepherd's cottage stands on the hillside within a stone's-throw, and here, years back, I recollect as if it were but yesterday asking for a glass of milk. It was a blazing day in August, and I had been fishing the Barle, with a college friend, from its source to Landacre. The time in those Oxford days was very sunny, for the mists of disappointment and sorrow were as yet afar. Often enough in the intervening years I have longed to revisit Exmoor, and at length, my wish fulfilled, find that the place has lost none of its former fascination. The loneliness of its

Wild Exmoor

hills and valleys does not depress me; on the contrary, my spirits are elevated, for the moors seem to contain a very elixir of life.

The heather is always beautiful, even before summer, with her lavish hand, has made the hillsides purple with it, and the stream is ever a companion. At this time of year there is, of course, a scarcity of animal life. A few stonechats and wheatears, just arrived, chatter and flirt their tails amidst the rocks; and the dipper or water-ousel forces attention by persistently curtsying to you from a boulder in mid-stream. He is a delightful fellow, this dipper, full of quaint sly ways; and by sitting quite still and watching, you may soon learn the ins and outs of his life. He comes and goes briskly from rock to rock, curtsying from every one, and uttering now and then a clear shrill whistle. I have often thought of the contrast between the modes in which man and the lower animals feed. The former has for the most part his stated hours for feeding, and partakes of his food with more or less punctuality. Take, on the other hand, the dipper—he has scarcely a spare moment while there is light, but is continuously seeking for food, earning his bread by the constant sweat of his brow.

Snipe, curlews, and partridges are fairly common on the moors; and the blackcock is plentiful in the neighbourhood of the Doone Valley. I saw on Exmoor, too, the ring-ousel, a very local species. Rabbits are plentiful, and, as a consequence, stoats and weasels. Herds of Exmoor ponies run wild; and in the Bagworthy Valley and neighbourhood you may sometimes see that grand animal, the wild red-deer.

There are three streams all rising hard by Simonsbath—the Barle, the Exe, and Bagworthy Water: the last-named, which flows through the Bagworthy Valley, is perhaps the most beautiful; but then, after passing Doone Valley and the idyllic Waterslide—rendered classic ground by Mr. Blackmore in his 'Lorna Doone'—the scenery changes entirely:

Wild Exmoor

the wild and treeless moors disappear, and the stream, uniting with the Lyn, flows on to the Severn sea through scenes, it is true, of surpassing loveliness, but wanting in the stern grandeur of the moorland: past Brendon village, and past Watersmeet, the scene in Whyte-Melville's 'Katerfelto' of the fierce struggle between Parson Gale and John Garnet: on to Woodside cottage and Lynmouth village, where, as Southey said, the river and the sea 'make but one sound'! Very pleasant memories these places have for me; but it is to Exmoor I would go when weary for a while of the sounds and sights of city life. A gracious silence broods over hill and valley, broken only here and there by the brawling of silvery trout-stream, and sometimes in the summer by the thunder echoing from hill to hill.

CHAPTER XI

Splitcane's Awakening

VISITING the pool Between-the-Willows in mid-winter, when the wind whistles through the brown, lifeless stems of the reeds and willow-herbs, you would surely fail to understand the fascination which it exercises in the fishing season over ardent anglers. The pool is scarcely a hundred yards from the highroad, and in a most exposed position. Along this road, in summer, many drags heavily laden with trippers pass daily on their way to Haddon Hall. One and all they are packed with folk who usually do most delight to aggravate the harmless fisherman, and to make day hideous in various ways. Clearly, therefore, the pool Between-the-Willows is a spot to be shunned by the

Splitcane's Awakening

angler who desires to be alone, or at least sequestered from the attention of rude fellows and bold hussies.

Thus might a man argue who had not seen the spot in its summer dress; and there is no denying that it has a bleak, disconsolate look after winter has committed his many crimes, and laid low to a leaf all the foliage of the beautiful willows and all the dense vegetable life of the river's brink. The author of 'My Old Village' warns us never to revisit the happy scenes of our youth. If we do, we shall find everything changed for the worse, and nothing but our own sad ghosts to meet us by all the hedges. It is almost equally depressing to revisit the favourite haunts by one's favourite stream in the depth of winter when the sundial is all shadow. Most appalling is the rack and ruin of the river-side.

Thus the pool Between-the-Willows seems in winter to have not a point in its favour. In addition to its exposure to every curious eye, it is little less than a raging torrent, for

Wye is bank-full and even brimming over. But how widely different is this spot in summer-time! In April it is still inclined to be bleak and unattractive; before May is well advanced the angler begins to stop and search its backwaters for rises, and by midsummer it is a jungle of sweet, flowering, growing things. Then the fisherman can tarry there in charming seclusion, hearing and seeing the trippers on their way to and from Haddon, but himself secure from all intrusion. The two old willow-trees, the high willow-herbs which form a regular hedge by the brink of the stream, the tall and softly waving meadow-grasses of June, and the thousand thousand other glorious green things of the lusty season—these all combine to shelter him from the curious gaze of the tripper. One of the willows has a kindly root high and dry above the water, and on this the angler can sit and scan every nook and corner of the backwater.

One season the pool was reported to have 'gone off' a little. It scarcely yielded its twenty brace of good trout, and there were rumours, too, that some black, ill-conditioned grayling had found their way thither, and were monopolising the best situations. I never could bring myself, however, to believe such tales against the pool. Even if it had 'gone off' for a while, the pool must re-stock itself with strong, wary trout, for it was always full of fly, and where the fly was, there also would be the fish.

Firmly believing like myself in the pool, my friend Splitcane continued to visit it each day during the summer fishing holiday. He more than glanced at it in the morning —a bad time of day for the pool—spent a quarter of an hour there at the least every afternoon; and on his way home in the evening would sit on the root for double that time, and always expect to see next minute the rise of a really big trout.

One afternoon he did actually see something which fairly staggered him. In the far corner—the deepest, most mysterious place in the pool—a gentle backwater crept between the bank and a mass of rubbish, which, arrested by a dead branch of one of the willows, had formed a regular platform. Curiously enough, a good rise had not been seen here during the season, though it looked the very place for one; but every one agreed that something which would probably turn the scale at four pounds must frequent the spot, even though it never rose to the fattest of olive duns or juiciest of may-flies. For a full hour the fish rose steadily, taking every olive that passed over it, but—another sure sign of something very large—never deigning to look at those which sailed a foot to right or left, or which coquetted with the water with many flutterings, after the manner of some freshly hatched fly. There was no splash or commotion; everything was done in that orderly, dignified style that is thoroughly characteristic of something very large among fishes. Splitcane hammered and he hammered, but to no effect. The fish treated all his pet patterns of duns and fancy flies with contempt; never rose at one of them,

Splitcane's Awakening

never even came to peer suspiciously at one of them. Each refusal added quite an ounce to the size of the fish in the imagination of the angler.

Splitcane was not one of those surly pot-hunters who keep quiet about the whereabouts of a good trout; so after dinner at the inn he told us all about it. Every one knew the exact spot in a moment from Splitcane's description, and next day most of us went to have a look, and, if the trout were 'up,' a try. The fish had come fairly on to the rise, and continued to take small and big olives on and off every day for a week. Thousands of artificials were sent over him, but all in vain. When Splitcane was seen approaching the pool, it was deemed the right thing for any one fishing there to give way to him. The curious thing was that this mysterious trout was never seen even in the most indistinct way.

He rose once, and once only, to the artificial on the sixth day. This was after Splitcane had spent altogether not less than twenty-four hours at the pool, left several gut-casts in the willows, used up some dozens of perfectly dressed olive and other flies, and broken two top joints. When Splitcane got hung up in the willow-herbs he would crawl through the wet grass like a reptile, and withdraw his hook with infinite care in order to avoid scaring the fish. As regards this single rise—it was one of Splitcane's friends who saw the dark deed done. A Sheffielder swinging carelessly along happened to see the fish rise, and cast his line, with two huge flies attached thereto, down stream. The fish rose, and was killed. Splitcane's friend begged the Sheffielder as a great favour to exchange the trout for one of about one and a-half pounds which he had in his own creel. The man good-naturedly agreed.

That evening, upon Splitcane's return to the inn, all his friends met him at the door. You should have seen his face when he heard that the trout had been taken—envy, malice, and all uncharitableness were depicted thereon. But you should have seen his face when

Splitcane's Awakening

a huge dish was brought out by two of the maid-servants into the hall, and the green stuff which had been placed over the trout to keep it fresh removed! There lay the mysterious trout. No wonder the Sheffielder had gladly exchanged it for a fat pound and a-half trout. It was about seven inches long, and as thin as a baby jack.

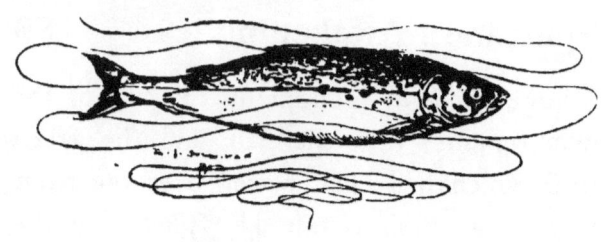

CHAPTER XII

A May Day's Angling

MANY anglers who resort regularly every season to Scotland, Wales, or so far afield as Norway, for their fortnight or three weeks of fishing, are apt to suppose that there is no first-rate fishing within easy distance of London; or, indeed, in the south country at all, save on those famous streams, the Test and Itchen. Yet there is probably very little, if any, trouting in Britain or Norway to surpass that which is obtainable by the fortunate few on a score or so of streams within an hour's rail of London. The Test, Itchen, and Kennet may be pre-eminent in reputation among South of England trout-streams. But the Chess, the headwaters of the Lea, and the little

A May Day's Angling

Mimram—the merest babbling brook in its upper portions—are scarcely less esteemed by those who know all these waters well than the more famous chalk streams of Hampshire and Berkshire.

One delightful day out of many such loitered away on a stream in a peaceful district in Hertfordshire somehow always stands out clear and vivid in my memory, though the bag was a very modest one indeed. This is a beautiful stretch of the clearest and least polluted water, and so easily reached that one may actually leave town after lunch, if a whole day be not available, and after three-quarters of an hour on that estimable line, the Great Northern, and twenty minutes' drive from the station, be, rod in hand, in the sweetest and quietest of meadows. One may get one's brace or perhaps several brace of trout, averaging at the least a pound—for there is a twelve-inch limit—and be back in town to dinner. On one occasion—in May 1892—in the excellent company of a north-country angling friend who came to 'carry the net' and watch the sport, I succeeded, more by luck than skill, in putting together a total bag of seventeen and a-half pounds of trout in the course of the afternoon, five of the fish scaling exactly one and three-quarter pounds apiece, which was, and I think still is, the record out of may-fly time on that water. But on this particular May day I had no friend to help me carry the net or fish, and as it so turned out did not greatly need assistance. I started forth intent above all things on loitering away the whole of a long day by the stream. The word 'loiter' may have an evil sound in the ears of some painfully laborious folk, but not so surely in those of Izaak Walton's true disciples, for did not the grand old angler boast of his desire to loiter whole days by Shalford Brook? A whole day at this time of year spent in the meadows restores, re-invigorates, physically and mentally; a few hours are too little for the purpose. Richard Jefferies found that he could not shake off

A May Day's Angling

the dust and din of town life, the oppressive sense of the great city, until he had reached a spot situated at a considerable distance from even the outskirts of London. Wandering in its vicinity, even in the greenest and peacefullest of lanes, he was irresistibly drawn towards the unrestful city as by a magnet. Others find, I think, that it is not so much distance as time which they require to get clear of the grip of London.

Half an hour after alighting from the train, I was on the look-out for rising trout, having driven a couple of miles through a typical piece of Hertfordshire scenery and through a cloud of dust — the one drawback to a fresh and brilliant May morning. The stream might be deemed scarcely worthy of a name by those who swear by the great rivers of the north country; just a quiet-flowing brook, often easily hidden behind a slender hedge, and, save here and there by some little white mill, rarely breaking into very audible music. With wading-stockings on you may cross it almost anywhere without risking a wetting, and draw out your fly from the sedge or willow on the opposite bank, to which, no matter how skilful you be, the hook will now and then attach itself. The water is so transparent that the tiniest of objects may be seen on the gravelly bed in places where the weeds are few and far between. This being so, it is easy to understand why the trout see the angler, or even the thin shadow cast by his rod, at a long distance off, and rush off to scare their neighbours, causing in the very shallow spots quite 'a wash' by the waves they make.

I found nobody on the water on my arrival. The fishing-hut, a compact little wooden structure, whither the members of the club repair for tea in the summer afternoons when nothing is doing, was locked, and looking round I could see no sign of human life or activity in all the meadows or in rich corn-lands above. I was alone amid the gently sloping hills and the little green valleys that prescribe to hard-worked Lon-

A May Day's Angling

doners the best of all medicines, peace. The meadow-grass was somewhat cruelly browned as though by the scorching heat of August; but the hedges were brilliantly green as at midsummer, with the oaks bursting forth into their full splendour of foliage. A hillside coppice hard by the stream was carpeted with wild hyacinths, and here and there in the open great marsh marigolds dared the heats and rainless days of a summer in spring.

Thus everything combined to make a pageant for a dweller in a towered city to feast his eyes and mind upon. But none of these things combined to make a good fishing day. The trout, it was true, were here in abundance, but lying in a sulky or slothful frame of mind at the bottom of the stream, and ignoring utterly the few olive duns which sailed jauntily down in the sunshine, and an occasional alder-fly which fell on the water and seemed bent on attracting the attention of its enemies by helpless flutterings. Nevertheless I strolled up stream quite contentedly—as who would not on such a day?—and almost reached the mill, beyond which my card of permission did not entitle me to go, before discovering a rising fish. At a bend in the stream almost forming a right angle a fish was busy well under the bank and in perilous proximity to a thorn-bush laden down to the water's brink with its great white clusters. After a few attempts I managed to get my fly floating and nicely cocked over the dimpling one. He bolted up and then down stream, and as a last resource dived into a patch of emerald-green weeds. But it was all of no avail; for he presently came to creel, a short, thick-set fish, just turning the scale at a pound.

And that, be it admitted, was the one sizable trout landed during the entire day. Three and four brace have been fairly common bags with me on this dainty stream; and in may-fly season, which occurs, as a rule, during the last few days of the month, much bigger baskets are, I believe, occa-

A May Day's Angling

sionally put together. Yet there was not much cause for disappointment, though a brace more would certainly have been acceptable. The walk to the station in the cool of the evening, when, for some reason or other, there is rarely a rise on this stream, was full of delight. The weird, but far from unpleasant, 'churn' of the goat-sucker was a sound to stop now and again to listen to; the nightingale rang out his passionate-seeming notes, 'liquid-sweet,' from all the coppices; and the air was redolent with the scent of many blossoms.

CHAPTER XIII

A Great Hatch of Fly

THE biggest hatch of fly I ever recollect seeing was on a misty day, with an overcast sky, in May 1892. The place was the Rutland length of the Derbyshire Wye, and the time the early afternoon. The olive dun came on in vast quantities. It floated down the stream, not in companies of half a dozen, such as one often sees when there is a good hatch of fly, but in companies of half a hundred or so. All our favourite backwaters were covered with the fly a quarter of an hour or twenty minutes after the hatch had commenced. It came not indeed 'single spies, but in battalions.' The trout and the grayling went mad, and remained so for an hour or an hour and a-half. In backwaters and other places, where one could not recollect having previously seen more than one trout feeding at the same time, there were two or three up. I had the Rutland length to myself that day, but took only a brace and a-half of fish, one of which was a dark, unattractive-looking grayling, and another a just-sizable trout killed *before* this phenomenal hatch began, or at any rate killed higher up stream, at a point where there was only now and again an odd dun or so sailing down. In fact, there was infinitely too much fly on the water to give the angler a chance of great sport. The artificial, when it alit on the water over a feeding trout—the fish lay for the most part close to the surface, and quietly sucked in the duns—was instantly in competition with a perfect swarm of live duns. Moreover, one was bound to lose sight of the artificial amongst this jostling crowd of natural insects, and, as a result, there was much striking on the chance of the rise being at one's own fly. The pool Between-the-Willows was a wonderful sight: in it there were at least twenty trout, all rising wildly at the duns without perceptibly thinning their numbers.

Almost as hopeless-looking as the bays and backwaters was the open stream, which was covered thickly with the insects. After rather wildly competing against these myriads of live flies in the backwaters and open stream near the willows, I hurried down, trying to find some spot not infested with the duns. To run away from the fly and from rising trout seems a strange thing for any dry-fly man to do, but it appeared on that day to be the one way of getting a few trout. I recollected a certain spot on the other side of the stream, which was, as a rule, a bad place for duns and rising trout. A willow laid one of its great dense boughs right across a considerable portion of the stream just above this spot, which would naturally prevent the fly coming down in numbers, save by a small channel on the opposite side of the water. Fly coming down would only filtrate slowly and with difficulty through the water-loving

A Great Hatch of Fly

foliage of this friendly old willow, and here, I reasoned to myself, I might find and kill some rising trout. Arrived at this spot, I found the fly coming down in moderate quantities—no duns ever seemed to actually hatch there—and speedily killed one beautiful fish, and hooked and lost another. Whilst I was considering where next to go, a friend who was not fishing that day came up, and excitedly pointed out half a dozen trout hard at it, a few paces down stream. He looked incredulous at the rather irritable reply of 'No good,' and begged me to try. I declined, and then, to his astonishment, and probably contempt, procceded with calm exterior, albeit with secret wrath and uncharitable feelings, to divest myself of my fishing-bag and take out lunch. Imagine a keen fisherman casting aside his rod and sitting down to lunch in the midst of a furious rise! The new-comer thereat seized the rod with scant ceremony, and, though he had no fishing ticket, commenced to assail first one, and then another, rising trout.

Half a dozen fish or so were up, one behind another in a line—a sort of Indian-file affair—and he tried them all. Whilst I munched my sandwiches and biscuits, for all the world as though it were the dead time of the day so far as trouting was concerned, he hammered away with increasing vigour but, as one could soon perceive, decreasing belief in his ability to fill the almost empty bag with trout. The sandwiches and biscuits disposed of, I turned my attention to the sherry-flask. In the days when Mr. Greaves still flourished in the famous old angling hostelry at Bakewell there was a renowned cellar. Every now and then we heard that in some unexplored corner of this cellar a rare old wine—

> ' whose father grape grew fat
> On Lusitanian summers '—

or a brandy worth a guinea a bottle, had been discovered and brought to light with the crust of a lifetime upon it. About this particular time a choice old brown sherry had been unearthed, and the same

A Great Hatch of Fly

was strongly recommended for consumption by dry-fly anglers off the premises. It was some slight consolation for the disappointment of that day. By the time lunch was well over, and a pipe lighted, the hatch had commenced to moderate, and the glutted fish began to drop out of sight as though ashamed of their orgies. Trout rose that afternoon in spots the most unlikely, and where it is ordinarily regarded by old Wye hands as idle to look for a feeding fish, whilst plenty of big trout, too, took up positions in the middle of the stream, and where the water flowed quite tumultuously, and sucked in duns, apparently as much at home as in their favourite backwaters. The hatch was over, so far as the fish were concerned, by about four o'clock, though long after that hour there was a good deal of fly floating down, dislodged no doubt from the eddies and backwaters of the stream. When the fish went down, they did so thoroughly. One might as well have looked for a good feeding fish on the highroad as in the river when the afternoon wore away—so complete was the reaction. A hatch of fly like the hatch of that day is worth seeing once; but that once goes a long way. The only other hatch of fly I have ever seen to in the least compare with it on a north-country stream was one of iron-blue duns, on a cold Sunday on the same river. The backwaters were covered with this most elegant little member of the *Ephemeridæ* family for an hour or two on that occasion, and the trout were suffered to enjoy a long and big meal unmolested. One often hears of great rises of the march brown in Devonshire streams, and the air is at times well-nigh blurred with the grannom over the waters of the Lambourne and the Kennet. A few seasons since, the may-fly hatched in such vast quantities on the Wye near Bakewell as to be a perfect pest. The insects were buzzing about the rooms of the inn and other houses in the town almost like house-flies in a confectioner's shop on a hot summer day.

CHAPTER XIV

The Thames Trout Fisherman

NEVER can Hurley backwaters seem lovelier to anglers, lovers, and boating folk than on placid August days. Beautiful beyond the power of words or of paint-brush to depict, on a Saturday, a Sunday, or even in the throes of a bank-holiday, how infinitely more are they so in the quiet of the week, on days as fair as that which Herbert hymned! The influx of boating men and women from London, and of non-boating men and women in boats, the crush at the locks, the pantings and screamings and steamings of the launches, the scatterings broadcast of pastry and pork-pie wrappers—these are the dreadfully familiar features which too often combine on high days and holidays to desecrate the stream which we Londoners have come to venerate as the Egyptians their Nile. But on the working days of the week the Upper Thames knows scarce a taint. The inmost recesses of the backwaters of Hurley may be seen at early morning in a virginal freshness; while in the evening, when the purple haze on the wooded hillsides is turning to grey, and the silence away from the weirs so supreme as to seem almost a thing to be grasped—material as the indescribable hum of the midsummer air — they may be converted by a slight effort of imagination into the untraced tiny tributaries of some Amazon of the New World.

But the professional Thames fisherman has not the time nor patience to let his mind slip away into such realms of fancy as these. He has only a few months every year, poor man, in which there is any real chance of getting hold of a trout that will screw his courage to the sticking-point, and try his tackle even to the middle joint of the rod. He has come

The Thames Trout Fisherman 107

out to try for a trout under and around the smallest and most beautiful fall of water at Hurley, and the blue haze on the hillsides, the 'woven caresses' of the trees over that long, delicious lane of water (emerald-green in certain lights), and the same thing where convenient of young men and maidens, are the merest details to him. He heeds them not.

The angler came round in a punt from the lock at about six o'clock on a still August evening. The sun had dipped behind the heights of Hurley, but it was still so warm that he sat in the punt with his coat off and his forearm bare. He was bronzed by perhaps many weeks' exposure to the river sun, which in a single day will, like a very furnace, scorch the skin off the face and even the arms of an unseasoned oarsman. In addition to being free of coat and waistcoat, he wore white flannels and tennis-shoes. There is no angler who understands, or who is able to carry out and enjoy, the art of keeping cool so well as the Thames trout fisherman. In the first place, he has nothing to carry; everything is in the punt within reach of his arm, from the jug of ale and stone bottles of ginger beer—which uniting make a froth white as the weir foam—downwards. Then the exercise necessitated is of the gentlest possible character; there is no fly-drying, and no hurrying along the bank when a big fish is hooked. Neither is he in his punt exposed to the jeers of passers-by, like the bank fisherman, nor to the frequent annoyance of a boat full of ill-natured Cockneys spoiling his best swim—treatment which in itself conduces to heat. Finally, he can moor his luxurious craft within reach of the delicious weir spray. Oh! enviable angler, if only the glory of the summer never wasted, and youth could perpetually replenish its stores, then you might sit and sit always, like Theseus, though unlike him know nothing save content!

The angler, however, knew that the summer evening—it being no longer June—would swiftly wane, so he lost no time in

The Thames Trout Fisherman

making his punt fast in the very roar of the waterfall. A few minutes later he tried his first cast. The bait, weighted to a nicety, was dropped softly into the water a yard or two from the fall, and quickly dragged down by the strong current into a comparatively gentle stream. The angler watched the line with intense interest and concern. When the current, not to be denied, had swept the bait into quiet water, he withdrew it and went through the operation again. Ten, twenty, fifty times was the bait withdrawn and replaced with a machine-like regularity, and yet the spirits of the fishermen were scarcely dashed. At the fiftieth cast he was still hopeful, and after it still unrewarded.

While he was removing a little bunch of weed from his hook a boat came round the bend, and threatened to invade the little bit of choice trout-water which the angler was doubtless congratulating himself on having found so secluded and unoccupied. Then, and not till then, he raised his eyes, saw fifteen yards beyond his punt, and with an unmistakable agony of gesture—his voice would have been lifted in vain in the roar of the weir—begged the intruders not to spoil his water. They instantly appreciated the situation and moored their boat at a respectful distance, where they could watch and hear the waterfall without interfering with the sport. There were two men and two pretty girls in the boat, and tea rather than trout was the object they had in view. The girls thought Thames trout-fishing must be very, very dull work, and could not understand how a man could possibly sit without agreeable companionship in a punt for hours together, angling for fish that never seemed to rise to the occasion. Fishing, indeed, is one of those things which few girls can understand. We sometimes read of ladies who have had great sport with the may-fly on Hampshire streams, or have landed big salmon on famous Scottish waters. But we rarely hear of one who will fish for hours at a stretch from a Thames punt, content with-

The Thames Trout Fisherman

out the ghost of a nibble—and that should be the test of a real Thames fisherman.

After two fruitless hours the angler unmoored his punt, and drifted down stream to a fresh spot, where no doubt with the same infinite patience he went through the same series of operations. It was long past seven o'clock then, and in the hour of the 'darkening leaf' the bat was already abroad. The little party of four had packed up their tea-things, and, unloosening their boat, which had only been held by a strong thistle now brought low to the water surface, glided away towards Temple. In the oily-smooth backwater the keel of the boat left a silver streak behind it, which, to match the utter hastelessness of nature, took whole minutes to fade away.

There was scarcely an hour of light left for angling. Yet no sooner had the patient and unrewarded angler left his station than three other enthusiasts came on the scene, and lost not a minute in casting their baits into precisely the same spot. There was a chance that the trout—a 'ten-pounder,' which had been seen several times in this place in July—though he had not stirred all day, so far as the bait was concerned, might come on the feed between eight and nine o'clock. The Thames trout fisherman —who often goes a whole season without taking a sizable fish—like love, believeth and hopeth all things.

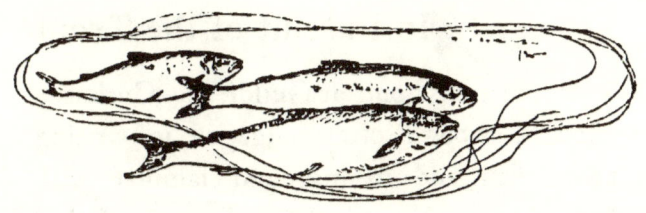

CHAPTER XV

Crichmere Memories

A HARD task it is to put upon paper all the little details that combine to make some of the most delightful open-air days of our life. It needs a far more skilful pen indeed than this to depict in black ink the glories of Crichmere and the wooded beauty of Haslemere on a fine summer's day; the eye and mind can scarce take them in, much less the unskilful hand portray them many months afterwards when midsummer has long since slipped away. 'If you see a fat little man, with his cap stuck full of flies, it will be Thomas Andrews'; so wrote the master of Crichmere in an invitation to me to come down to Haslemere one June day, inspect the ponds, and afterwards travel back and dine

H

with him at his home at Guildford. Curiously enough, though often engaged in writing about fish and fishing, and familiar with Mr. Andrews' methods and work, I had never been fortunate enough to meet him. I therefore made a point of starting early from Waterloo in order to get as long a day as possible at Haslemere and Guildford. Even the journey by rail from London to Haslemere, at least during the last ten miles or so, is a treat. Tiny copses alternate with green meadows; sweet villages nestle on either side of the line and amidst the pleasant hills of Hants and Surrey. A fly was waiting at Haslemere station, which conveyed me along a road, or call it a lane, such as only the South of England can show. In the tall, straggling hedges grew profusely the wild-roses, those most delicate of blossoms, which, like Shelley's narcissi, when gathered and made a nosegay of, seem to 'die of their own dear loveliness.'

Out of this shady road-lane led a woodland path, and here, waiting for me, was the

Crichmere Memories

'little fat man' with the flies in his cap. Though only acquainted through correspondence, we were friends in five minutes, and, of course, hard at it spinning fishing yarns. Did I fish? Dry fly—good. Where? Derbyshire, Kent, Hertfordshire — better. Of course, he knew all the streams and their fishes; many of the latter, indeed, were near blood-relatives to the trout I had come down to this place to see. 'You haven't brought your rod,' said Mr. Andrews, 'so I shall have to lend you one, because I want to put you on to a six-pounder, which is usually anxious to get a hook into its mouth.' I immediately wanted to be put on to that trout, but my companion intimated quietly, though firmly, that the first thing to do was to have lunch, the second to see the ponds and their inhabitants, and the third to get back to Guildford. The particular six-pounder referred to was not here at all, but at the back garden at Westgate House. Crichmere itself has been so constantly described that I shall content myself with remarking that its position is an ideal one, not only from the point of view of the pisciculturist, but also from that of the worshipper at the shrine of nature in her most self-assertive and untrammelled state. The making of the fish-ponds, and the erection of a small wooden building or two, have, indeed, in no way spoilt this fair spot. Lavish vegetation has not only been permitted, but actually encouraged, in order to ensure the conditions of the fish-life being as natural as possible, and also to get a good supply of the usual food of trout in a wild state.

We turned into a snug little hut, where my host at once set about laying the table for lunch. The utensils were a couple of pocket-knives, a cup, and a flask. Tablecloth, forks, glasses, and luxuries of this kind we neither had nor required. The angler does not take such things out with him on his excursions, and we, if not actually on angling bent, were, as I presently discovered, at any rate amongst the rising trout, and could, therefore, very well put up with

Crichmere Memories 117

a rough fishing picnic. Mr. Andrews produced a small loaf, broke it in two, gave one half to me and kept the other; likewise did he equitably divide the butter, the cheese, and a slice or two of pressed beef. We fell-to, sitting at the bare, but scrupulously clean, board. As we sat at table the sunshine came in at the window, steeping the wooden hut in beauty and delight; whilst through the wide-open door stole a light breeze fresh from the pure heights of the Surrey hills. After lunch there arose the inevitable aroma of tobacco, and then it was, as later when wandering amongst the ponds, that Mr. Andrews did hold forth concerning the common trout—a creature on the whole not undesirable, but at times, it must be admitted, so perverse that many anglers have been known to use against it very questionable English.

During a considerable part of my life I have been prying into the habits and haunts of the fish, and noting its aggravating ways when angled for; but I soon found that my knowledge and observation were as a few drops in a trout-stream compared with Mr. Andrews'. Either as a pisciculturist or an angler, Mr. Andrews thought trout, spoke trout, wrote trout, and caught trout at all seasons of the year. I could wish that he had left some notes to hereafter supply the naturalist with material wherewith to write a really accurate life-history of the trout; it is the zeal and unwearied observation of men like the late owner of Crichmere that make scientific natural history possible. In a way he was the Gilbert White of the fishing world. Now and again the sporting instinct would predominate with Mr. Andrews, and at such times he must fish somewhere, even in his own ponds. In one of these ponds were, and are, a score of show fish not averaging under six pounds apiece. Here, on more than one occasion, the pisciculturist turned angler, and had a set-to with one of his own pets, which rose at a big sedge or alder fly.

My mind to-day is still full of memories of our wanderings at Crichmere, and my

Crichmere Memories

host's angling stories on the way back to his pleasant home at Guildford, with its quaint old garden on the banks of the Wey. 'Let's see,' said Mr. Andrews meditatively when we arrived there on the softest of summer evenings, ' he says he only fishes dry fly. Now (turning to me), you heard of those five and six pounders I recently put into the river? Well, they are always hanging about at the end of the garden. Would you like to have a try? My little girl got broken in one the other day.' Then he went down amongst the scarlet-runners with a spade and a flower-pot filled with moist moss, and proceeded to dig. After which, I went a-dryfly-fishing—the method being by float and lob-worm. I know that I ought not to have done it; but it was the only sin I committed through the live-long summer day. I think that those who spent much time with Mr. Thomas Andrews, of Crichmere, were as little likely to err seriously as Walton or his friend Herbert.

CHAPTER XVI

The Great Unlanded

THE biggest fish are always lost. It is almost a platitude to say so. But it is the lost fish which, in a way, gives the true angler his keenest delight, just as it gives him also his greatest pain. It is a severe trial at the time, and for a short while afterwards, the losing of a heavy fish, the fish of the day, of the season, perhaps even of a lifetime. You return a dejected and, in cases where you have blundered, a shamed man. It is not until you have had dinner or supper, and have blown forth some fragrant clouds of the soothing herb, that you can narrate the appalling incident to your brother-anglers with anything like a calm and unruffled demeanour. Yet it is these very losses which in the end

The Great Unlanded

may give the greatest pleasure. Every incident in connection with the stalking, hooking, and playing of a big fish which is not landed will be remembered and pondered over months, even seasons, afterwards with something like relish. The histories of your captures are comparatively soon blurred over and forgotten. Just as the most beautiful trout that Kennet or Wye ever yielded soon loses its perfect colour and form when taken from its element, so does the memory of these victories, after the first flush, often grow dim and cold.

Some of the fish which are hooked and lost are never seen, or seen in the most indistinct manner. Their exact sizes remain a mystery, never to be cleared up, and mystery has a great fascination for the angler. Dark, deep holes amongst the gnarled roots of immemorial willows attract him vastly. If he goes to such places between the lights and suddenly sees a may-fly sucked under and a great telltale ring in its place, which expands till it faints away into the bosom of the stream, his whole being is stirred. His mind hastens to conceive of a fish so big and fierce that, if the same be hooked, the top joint simply must snap, the gut cast give, or the fifty yards of line run out and off the reel before the staggered fisherman has time to pull himself together and remember that there is no knot at the end. But fancy what the feelings of the angler must be if such a mysterious monster is actually hooked in a place like this, and played for a few seconds before the inevitable smash amongst the snags comes! That trout may weigh anything in the mind of the angler up to, say, seven pounds or eight pounds, though no fish has ever been taken out of the stream heavier than five pounds. Perhaps he takes a friend or two to see the spot next day. They no longer doubt, if they did so overnight ; the fish must have been a regular demon. Years afterwards that short, sharp struggle is recalled as vividly as though it had just happened. The time and the place are engraved indelibly on the memory. It may be that they will even be

The Great Unlanded

remembered when the first kiss of first and only love is forgotten. Other good fish may have been hooked and landed about that very time, and almost that very place. But memory spurns them. In previous chapters I have told the tales of several of my misfortunes or blunders, where heavy trout have been concerned; but those are only a few among many similar disasters.

A huge tree has fallen right across my favourite stream in the north country. Its mighty roots, torn up savagely from the kindly earth, stretch themselves indignant to the skies, and the water, here swift and strong, rushes with sound and fury over the trunk and through the thick branches, some of which were still putting forth leaves last summer. Masses of river wreckage have accumulated amongst the branches, which have grown so burdened and weighty that presently a winter flood will, sweeping down, whirl the whole fabric away. A great trout came and took up his abode in a backwater or eddy immediately below this tree. He was there at Easter, and again in August. In the full light of day his wariness knew no bounds; and as there was a nasty drag, the artificial fly was drowned almost the moment it touched the water. He would not look at nor think of such a base imitation of the olive; indeed, the fastidious monster, dimly seen sometimes by myself who watched him, as through a glass darkly, picked and chose his natural olives. He appeared now and then to take a fly as a mere sauce or appetiser for other and more solid food. It was his sherry-and-bitters before dinner. But once, at about eight o'clock in the evening, I passed the tree on my way home, and found him gorging on natural fly, which was on in large quantities. I waited not an instant, but cast my fly almost amongst the twigs of the fallen tree and let it float over him. He rose, but, owing evidently to the drag, declined. The water being very low, I resolved to wade out into the stream and take up my position immediately below the fish, and on a bed of almost dry gravel. In this manner the drag would

The Great Unlanded

be avoided. No sooner thought of than accomplished. At the first cast he came at the fly with a will and was hooked. A desperate attempt to get amongst the twigs of the tree failing, he came down with a furious rush almost under my feet. The winch sang a merry, merry tune. Thirty yards of line were out before I realised the position. I understood it better when the line came back and the top of the rod straightened itself out! I never saw him except in a dim and distant manner, but I cherish the belief that he was the kind of fish which is ultimately choked by trying to swallow a drowned puppy. Even the other night I seemed to hear once more the song of the reel, and to feel the rod bend like a bow as by a clean-run salmon in its first rush.

There is another spot to which my thoughts revert even more persistently. This is an osier-bed by the Kennet. The stream is full of coarse fish, and the trout only rise in this part of the river when the may-fly is on. If a dozen are taken during that period, the season is regarded as a good one, and it is customary to put back anything under about three pounds. A five-pounder is a good, but not an exceptional, fish. The keeper knew the osier-bed well, and explained to me the exact quarters of something very big, which he had seen thinning the drake on the previous day. So I pushed my way through, and, creeping to the edge of the river, looked with feverish interest at the water as it curled in an oily way round some huge dock-leaves. If ever there were a place for a heavy trout, this was it. It was secluded to a degree, unassailable from any spot save where I lurked, all eyes; a deep pool, but not too sluggish, and with abundance of rank herbage, which big fish affect. Still, though I waited and watched long, no sign of a fish was vouchsafed. The beauty of the day wore on, and the sun began to dip behind the trees in its westering course. May-flies slid over the water, caught against the stems of the docks, were whirled into every eddy, and, drifting back into the open stream, sped on-

The Great Unlanded

ward untouched. But by and by, when the sunlight died off the water, a fly sailed down to the spot on which my eyes still rested, and then suddenly disappeared without a splash, without even a ring. It seemed drawn underneath by some overmastering current. My own fly alit on the water a second or so later—a clumsy cast, fully two feet from the spot where the drake came by its death and right out of the eddy. But just as I was about to remove it with self-reproach from the water a dark form loomed up from the depth and broke the surface of the water. My heart stood still, but my wrist moved, and then there was a mighty splash and a vicious pull. The treacherous gut gave instantly, and the dark form sank from sight. Nothing would ever convince me that that osier-bed trout was an ounce under eight pounds. The keeper put him down at seven, but then the keeper had not felt that mighty pull. No, I shall continue to believe that a good eight pounds was his weight. Fish of that weight have been taken from the

Kennet, and the osier-bed pool was of all spots the one which would be inhabited by the biggest trout of all.

It is a cruel thing, and an unnecessary thing, to destroy these dear delusions, for such no doubt they frequently are. Sometimes we do so ourselves by obstinately returning again and again to a fish we have hooked and lost. Finally we hook and land the fish, and are disgusted to find that it is not much more than sizable. Such things have occurred, even in the case of the most experienced and adroit anglers. Splitcane is not the only angler I know who has been cruelly disillusioned. A friend told me last season that he spent the best part of two long days throwing over what he took to be a very heavy trout by its quiet, businesslike rise at olive duns, and that he eventually discovered it to be about six inches long. Fortunately these painful disclosures are only occasional. As a rule, when we lose our unseen fish we are permitted to believe that a very monster has escaped the landing-

The Great Unlanded

net or the gaff, as the case may be. Our struggle accordingly assumes heroic proportions, and passes into the history of our lives as anglers. It is recorded in the smoking-room of the inn to brother-anglers and brother-sufferers, and they in turn recount their similar experiences. Let all fishermen acknowledge and be thankful for the precious gift of imagination which is meted out to them in such a generous measure. Let them also rejoice to think that every fish hooked is not brought to basket, for in the great unlanded may lie one of the many charms of the angler's art.

CHAPTER XVII

The Darenth in June

SURELY the most delicious of all angling months is that of the Midsummer. Even if it be often enough the season of low water, and bright sunshine throughout the greater part of the day, it offers ample compensations to the trout fisherman in many other respects. There is no time when the meadows and stream-side are more delicious, after, perhaps, a tramp of a mile or two along the dusty highroad, than at this period of the year. The evening fishing is not yet in its prime, it is true, but then there is

The Darenth in June

often a fairly steady rise all day, whereas later on in the season the afternoon is apt to be entirely barren of sport. Then there is still observable throughout a considerable part of this month a great deal of bird life—in which most anglers take an interest—though it is not the teeming life of early May, when the summer visitors are noisily settling down to their nesting operations.

A three-mile walk from Swanley one June day last season to a little stretch of the Darenth in which I was entitled to fish would have been perhaps more agreeable had it not been for the dust, fine as flour, which every passing cyclist—and the wheeling folk on Kent highroads at holiday-time may be numbered by tens of thousands—stirred up in clouds. The excessive dustiness of the roads is, indeed, one of the chief drawbacks of hop and strawberry land for the cyclist or pedestrian. It tends to lessen to his view

> 'All the pensive glory
> That fills the Kentish hills.'

Once in the water-meadows, however, one speedily shakes off any slight sense of oppression and disgust caused by the whirling dust of the roadside. Here the deep green of June can never weary the eye, any more than the low tunefulness of the brook can the ear.

It is pleasant to find fish rising honestly to the fly directly one reaches the water-side. This was the case upon arrival at the Darenth, which I had not visited since an uproarious day during the preceding month, when to try to fish was to make sure of losing one's temper together with many flies. The Darenth is not by any means a stream naturally adapted to fly-fishing in all its most fishful lengths. On the contrary, it is aggravatingly wooded at some of the best points. My first fish was rising in the steady, methodical way of trout when they are in next to impossible places. He was right under the opposite bank, and shaded by a large dock which drooped down to the water and formed a nice natural umbrella.

The Darenth in June

To get to him it was necessary to cast through a couple of willows on my side of the bank, and to cast underhanded; not a pleasant business at all, especially as the fly, when it did alight fairly near the fish, was almost certain to be drowned by the 'drag.' Half a dozen times, perhaps, he came after the fly—a darkish olive dun—and once or twice broke the water, without getting hooked. The fly was then changed, and a bright little 'governor,' often very effective in Hertfordshire, substituted.

Ultimately I returned to the olive dun, and had just resolved, after half an hour's hard work, to give it up as a bad business, when the fish followed the fly down for perhaps the eighth or ninth time, rose, was hooked, and rushed into a bed of weeds. Some anglers advise a loose line in the case of a fish that has 'weeded' you, and others say on no account fail to keep your line taut. Inclining to the latter in this instance, I held on for about five minutes, when out he came, and played as though just hooked.

The Darenth fish seemed to me to be extremely game the whole of last season, and one game trout of a trifle under a pound taken the same day made the reel sing quite a merry song for a few seconds, though the water was neither deep nor strong. The may-fly was on in small quantities throughout the day, and especially in sunny intervals after a refreshing shower or two, but the fish would not look at the perfect insect, though many of them in the evening were 'bulging' at the larvæ; they preferred the modest little dun, and an occasional 'curse,' or midge.

Two brace of trout in admirable condition, the smallest over half a pound, and the largest about a pound and a quarter, form only a very moderate bag for the Darenth about may-fly time; but their weight is apt to be appreciated when added to the rest of the angler's impedimenta in the course of a three-mile walk to the station after a hard afternoon and evening's work. Moreover, the primary object of fly-fishing

The Darenth in June

is not mere slaughter. The capture of each of these four fish is a little history in itself, which affords food for agreeable thought on the way back to town. When the bag is heavy, it is difficult, even a few hours afterwards, to recall the incidents in connection with the taking of each trout, and triumph is apt to give place to satiety.

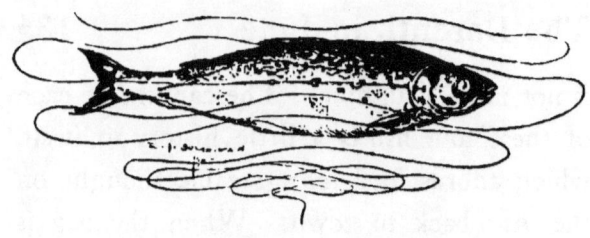

CHAPTER XVIII

A Question of Heredity

'Much information respecting the habits of aquatic insects can be extracted from anglers by those who speak their language,' says Professor Miall in his 'Natural History of Aquatic Insects.' If this is true in regard to the flies that trout devour, it is even more so in regard to the trout. There have been natural histories of the trout and to spare from a non-angling point of view written during the last few years, but not one of them has attempted to deal at all thoroughly with the exceedingly interesting question of whether the trout of to-day are really wiser than their forebears, and whether, if they are wiser, their increased sagacity is hereditary or merely acquired by each trout through bitter experience of the hooks and the mani-

A Question of Heredity

fold wiles of the angler. Does the excessive cunning of a knowing old trout in Test, Itchen, Derbyshire Wye, or Kennet die with him, or is it transmitted to future generations of trouts to keep light the creel and heavy the heart of the angler yet unborn? This is a question which no scientific man seems so far to have laid himself out to investigate; and, indeed, it may be doubted whether he could do so with a chance of arriving at the truth, unless a keen and observant angler himself, or else aided in his researches by a chalk-stream fisherman. The habits of that shyest of fish, the trout, can only be thoroughly understood by long and close observation on the banks of a clear and slow-flowing stream, and even then to get a really good idea of the fish's cleverness and sense of danger one must be a keen angler oneself.

That the trout of our chalk streams are much more difficult to impose upon with an artificial fly than of yore really cannot be questioned. There are *laudatores temporis acti*, it is true, who are always ready to deplore the falling-off in sport in all its branches, and it would be dangerous to trust too much in what such folk have to tell about the wonderful bags they used to make a quarter or half a century since. But there is plenty of reliable evidence in relation to these and other famous waters which points unmistakably to the fact that trout-fishing with a fly is a much more difficult and scientific business than it was a few decades ago. Colonel Hawker used to enjoy a good many days' fly-fishing in the course of the season, beginning early in spring and frequently angling on till late in September, and he nearly always obtained in the course of a few hours what the Test 'artist' of to-day would regard as a handsome dish of trout at even a very favourable season. His water was hard by Longparish, which remains to this day a famous spot for trout, and occasionally he tried a day on the Anton near Andover, or on the Test at Stockbridge. Here are a few of the many astonishing angling entries in his diary, taken haphazard: 'July 13, 1810. Caught fish by throwing the fly as I sat in the phaeton.' (In another place the colonel declares that it is as easy to kill fish from horseback as on foot!) 'May 27, 1807. Longparish. Killed twenty brace of trout with a fly in three hours.' 'May 13, 1847. Having a demand for fish, I brandished a fly rod. The trout were so sulky, owing to the cold storms, that it took me a long time to catch ten brace.' On another occasion he tells us that he went minnow-fishing in the dusk of the evening, and lost all the best time by having to send home for some fresh tackle, 'and on its arrival the first and only fish I caught with it was the very one which had just broken my line, and from whose mouth I pulled out my former hooks, gut, swivels,' etc. Longparish trout, killed by the ten-brace and the twenty-brace in the height of the season by an angler who thought nothing of fishing from his carriage or his horse's back, and who, as we know from his notes, used several sunk flies on a cast of not over-fine gut, and flogged away up, down, or across stream on chance! The thing sounds like a nightmare to the dry-fly angler of the Test, Itchen, or Wye of to-day; yet that Colonel Hawker's accounts are substantially true cannot fairly be doubted. He appears, moreover, to have enjoyed as remarkable sport at the end of the fifth decade of the present century as he did forty years earlier. In many stretches of these Hampshire chalk streams trout are to-day, in all probability, as plentiful and certainly as large as they were in Colonel Hawker's time; but what an extraordinary change has come over them! To fish from a phaeton would be to scare them well-nigh out of their senses for an hour or more; and to fish with a cast of the comparatively clumsy and ill-dressed flies of half or three-quarters of a century ago would be to put fish after fish off the rise. If you can 'set down' a rising trout by simply showing him an inch too much gossamer gut, or a tiny dun—exactly resembling the natural fly on the water—'dragged' unnaturally over his nose, how much more likely are you to offend these fastidious and highly educated fellows by tackle and lures such as the colonel was wont to brandish? Nor are the Test trout the only fish which have grown so mightily particular within, say, the last score of years. The trout of the Derbyshire Wye—of, that is to say, the lower and most constantly fished stretches of the stream—have, within the experience of even youthful anglers, developed the same characteristics; and those of certain fishful portions of the Kennet are, if anything, even worse from a creel-filling point of view. Colonel Hawker scarcely imitated nature at all, and yet he usually filled his creel whenever he chose: we imitate nature closely—so closely that even an experienced hand has occasional difficulty in distinguishing his own fly from the natural insect on the water—and yet we generally fail to half fill our creel.

Dry-fly fishing was resorted to on the Test,

Itchen, and other streams because anglers discovered that out of may-fly season they could kill trout by no other method of fly-fishing; and within the last ten years or so it has been adopted on the Derbyshire Wye for much the same reason. Undoubtedly the average trout has greatly increased in sagacity in these streams. The only question is, whether this added intelligence is of an hereditary kind or not. Professor Romanes, in his little work, 'Animal Intelligence,' touches the mere fringe of this question. His view is that 'the marked increase of wariness' in trout is the result of observations made by each trout for itself; but he does not seem to have very closely studied the matter, for he gives no good reason for arriving at such a conclusion. One writer stated it as his opinion, I believe, that it is scarcely possible for this intelligence to be transmitted, because the parent fish have no opportunities of teaching their young, as various birds and beasts have. Another writer—the late Mr. Andrews, I think—whose views on a

A Question of Heredity

subject of this kind were always worthy of the attention of naturalists as well as anglers, owing to his knowledge of pisciculture, and his careful observations of trout life, discussed the question in an article in 'Baily's Magazine' a few years since : 'Compare (he wrote) by analogy the fact, which is, I believe, well authenticated, that when first telegraph wires were stretched along our highroads the number of partridges and other birds which, in fair weather, and not driven by unusual force of gale, committed involuntary suicide by flying against the wires was very large, while in the present day such cases are comparatively unknown. This goes to prove a certain reasoning power on the part of the old birds and *an inherited capacity* for avoiding the danger by their progeny.' The theory of heredity in regard to the increased wariness of the common trout, though very far indeed from being proven, is quite one which scientific men and naturalists may treat seriously.

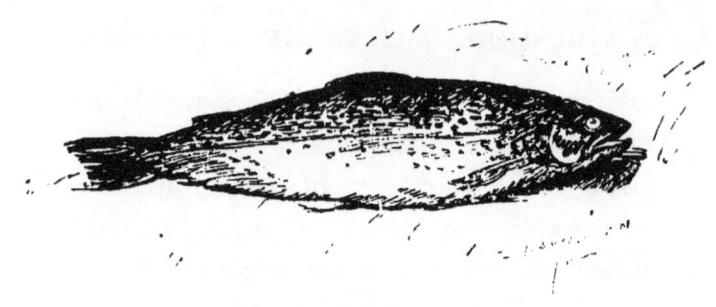

CHAPTER XIX

May-fly Dreams

MAY-FLY season comes almost before many of us—Londoners by profession, but anglers and countrymen by persuasion—have had time to grasp the fact that the youth of the year is getting to be middle-aged; that, by tradition at any rate, light-hearted sun-and-shower-mixt April, and May with lap full to overflowing of flowers and birds' eggs, are already 'portions and parcels of the dreadful past.' The song-thrush sings as well in many a London park, open space, square, ay, even small back garden, hard by the very busiest thoroughfare, as he does in the thickets and dingles of the Hampshire wood and common where my boyhood was, in matters others than those of mere study

May-fly Dreams 145

and thought for to-morrow, well spent; the lilac is of as lovely a colour and emits as delicious a scent in Buckingham Palace Road as it does in the thick shrubberies that surround the house in the midst of that wild wood. But we cannot afford to heed them more than a few times at the most before they are over. The unrest of London forbids us to dwell on these things, which tend to take our thoughts off the ever-engrossing concerns of city life. We just catch a glimpse of them much as a traveller in an express looks out from his carriage window to get his fifty-miles-an-hour glimpse of a pretty little orchard, a glittering trout-beck, an old, low, mossy church-tower, a patch of primroses in a thinly underwooded coppice feathering down to the line. We too often slight Nature in London, though of all spots in the world it might be supposed that in London her value should be most priceless.

Yet about may-fly season, ever when I cannot get away from town for a day or two's angling, my thoughts will very commonly be straying—to the detriment of business—to my ideal stream. I call it ideal, because I can never hope to angle in it; it is perfectly inaccessible to me, and indeed, as I have always understood from various inquiries, to the rest of the angling world. There is only a record of one person fishing there, and I have never been able to satisfy myself that he actually did so, though the villagers have a story to that effect. They also say that once a year the staff of servants employed by the absent owner of the stream and the mansion hard by are allowed a day and whatever baits they choose in may-fly time; but this story is getting more and more into disrepute, for nobody has ever been seen straying along the green velvet banks of that stream with a rod in his or her hand,—and this goes far to disprove the alleged permission to angle once a year accorded to one man—the parish pastor—and a staff of servants.

What is there so wonderful in this stretch of water? Why, simply this, that it is the

May-fly Dreams   147

most beautiful and the most likely-looking for big trout that the enthusiast ever dreamt of. I have often fished the water above, and several times, too, the water below, and have had some delightful trout out of both.

Below the trout run big, and you must really take the trouble of looking very carefully indeed to your gut about the time the spent gnat comes out. Above, again, there are genuine little flour-mills still working, things you read of in poetry, and watercress beds, and tiny bee-farms, and perfect hamlets of the kind you see as a rule only in Birket Foster's dainty pictures, and a real old English village—a village in the midst of 'poppy-mingled corn,' where

> 'Aylmer follow'd Aylmer at the Hall,
> And Averill Averill at the Rectory
> Thrice over.'

And there is a baker's in that village where they make the most wonderful bread. The door of the shop is always open at this time of year in the daytime, and as you pass you enjoy an aroma not easily forgotten. New bread in London gives me hideous indigestion; but I can eat it steaming hot from the oven there without its doing me the least harm. Well, these accessories in themselves help to make as it were a pleasant setting. But the stream itself, where it runs glimmering through the park that surrounds that mysterious old house, which is only visited once in every five years by its owner—what a picture it is! At one point, and at one only, can you get a peep at it from outside. A high and very thick hedge shuts out all view, save where the road crosses the stream. I cannot cross that bridge on my way from the quiet little station to the stretch of water a mile or so above, without leaning over for five minutes or so to see what is going on in the park with the 'immemorial elms' and oaks; and, if it be not too dark, I always take another peep coming back in the cool of the evening. The trees for a little way from the bridge form a regular avenue, uniting over the stream, which presently

May-fly Dreams

widens out into a shallow lake. How absolute the quietude there! One may see a wild-duck, or even a coot, on the water now and again, though the house is within a stone's-throw of the left bank. Sometimes in the distance a gardener may be seen working in the leisurely way that befits such a spot.

The stable clock seems to chime the 'slow, sweet hours' as leisurely as the gardener mows a bit of lawn or picks up a weed or two from the gravel drive up to the house. It may be years before the lord and master comes again to the old house for a few days: there is no need to hurry. No doubt the trout, too, are as leisurely as the gardener and the clock. But still there always appear to be a few fish moving, and occasionally one sees with a thrill of excitement a great tail waving gently out the stream, which it is natural to set down as pertaining to a four-pounder. Indeed, from what I have observed once or twice in may-fly time, and from what I have heard said by villagers who have known other villagers who have been in the park, there are some fearsome fellows in and near the lake. 'Do you think there is a six-pounder there?' I have unreasonably inquired of a water-keeper in a stretch some way above. 'That's a terrible big fish, sir,' was his reply, 'but I've a-heard say that it's a mighty fine water when the fly's up.' A six-pounder, well hooked, with the may-fly, and absolutely reliable gut—there is something almost solemn in the thought! But for my part, should the owner of that fishery ever take it into his head to send me permission to angle there in may-fly time, I shall be content to bring home, say, a brace and a-half of trout in perfect condition weighing nine pounds, and one fish turning the scale at five. This is one of my regular may-fly dreams.

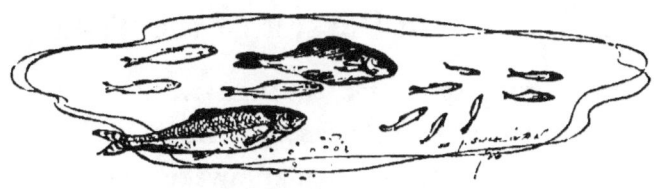

CHAPTER XX

A Visit to Troutbridge

For eleven months and a bit out of each twelve the little town of Troutbridge in Chalkshire sleeps.

It wakes up for about three weeks in June when the may-fly is on, but before midsummer it is dozing off again, and practically it will slumber serenely till the end of the following May.

Now and again on a bright winter day there is some faint sign of animation in the town when the hounds come through on their way to the regular three-times-a-year meet at the 'Pig and Whistle' hard by; and on the first of September there is something in the nature of a slight bustle about the Lion Hotel, where a little knot of sportsmen from town congregate for the first week of the partridge-shooting season. But you can scarcely call these regular awakenings; it is, on such occasions, only as though Troutbridge turned drowsily over in its bed and almost instantly got off to its profound slumber again.

How long the place has been sleeping I cannot say; perhaps since 1879, when the agricultural interest was first hit so hard; perhaps since the borough was robbed of its Parliamentary representation. Anyhow, in my boyhood Troutbridge always seemed to me, no matter what the season of the year, to be an extraordinarily bright and busy spot. It was the 'London' town of my youth.

Troutbridge, whether awake or asleep, is a charming angling resort. Within a hundred miles or so of town, and with a railway station, it is yet quite unspoilt by the gilt touch of progress. No factory has sprung up to mar with hideous chimney the quaint old architectural beauty of the town, and the shops, inns, dwelling-houses, and public build-

A Visit to Troutbridge

ings are exactly the same as they were when I first knew them, and thought they must be some of the finest in the country. Troutbridge lies in a very green and 'deeply meadowed' corner of Chalkshire, and its stream, the Clear, is of pure spring water. The Clear runs right through the town. Many of the cottages have their pleasant gardens adjoining it, and one may occasionally see, attached to a fruit-tree or bush, a tell-tale line swaying backwards and forwards in the current.

Over the red brick town bridge, when the fly is fairly up, you will usually see three or four of the inhabitants leaning and pointing out to one another, with an eagerness rare in the very easy-going men and women of Troutbridge and its district, the heavy fish which feed noisily at that point, and are not in the least shy of an audience. Sometimes an angler will stop and drift his artificial may-fly down to one of these trout, and when one is hooked what a commotion both above and beneath the bridge takes place!

But the angler is not, as a rule, wont to hang about the town bridge. He prefers a long day in the meadows of the Clear, and at no season of the year are these so inviting as in may-fly time, while the freshness of the summer still lingers. Before June has half gone, the youth and gaiety, the abandon, of the summer are in a way things of the past. The season is middle-aged and inclined to be staid. The warblers have ceased their songs by day and by night, save in a very few instances, and the foliage of even the latest trees has lost the tender verdure of spring. But at may-fly season the summer has scarcely lost any pleasant feature, and this is, on the whole, perhaps above all others the time to fully enjoy the river-side.

The may-fly is in these days often abused and described as the most disappointing of insects. 'It's been a bad may-fly season everywhere,' one has too frequently heard anglers declare, and certainly my own experiences have been of a rather disappointing character, so far as heavy bags at this time

A Visit to Troutbridge

of year are concerned. And yet I do not wonder that, despite the disposition to dash the hopes of young may-fly dreamers, Troutbridge inns fill up with keen anglers at this season, and the Clear is more severely assailed for ten days or so than during the remainder of the year. As I have tried to show, the attractions offered by the meadows are irresistible just now, and then, besides, trout, and very heavy ones too, do display a rare activity when the fly is fairly up.

Come with me to the aldered banks of the Clear, a quarter of a mile out of the town, and I will try to show you a very little of the stream and sport. When I last visited the Clear it was April. A howling northeast wind one day and a steady downpour the next were enough to take the edge off the pleasure of our first two days' trout fishing in 1897 in this stream. It is true that trout were rising pretty constantly at certain points where the surface food, duns, midges, and the like, congregated by reason of the wind, and that we started angling at ten o'clock both mornings, hurriedly lunched in sheltered spots, and did not leave the water till the oncoming of 'dark-hour.' But if the Clear had its attractions then, how much more does it draw us now, when the season is clothed and in her right mind, and it is possible, even tempting, in between the rises to lie down at some excellent spot and scan the water carefully for the ring or dimple which gives away the secret of the lair of a feeding trout! A little later on the may-fly will be out most of the day in its myriads, but now it seems to appear in only fair quantities at intervals of several hours, and I am not sure that this is not the best time for the angler. The trout, after partaking largely of the insect under water and before it has assumed its winged form, have turned their attention to the floating insect, and they are possibly a good deal keener than they will be in a few days' time after 'the glut.'

That bend yonder, where the stream, after a sluggish course of a hundred yards or so, breaks into a gentle current, strongest under

A Visit to Troutbridge

the opposite bank, which has been planted by Nature with a tall hedge of willow-herb, is a great place for the may-fly. Somehow the insect seems to hatch there more freely than at most other points; and if you do not mind going into the rushes on this side and feeling the water rush in over your boot-tops—for we do not allow waders on the Clear—you will presently see a fish or two 'up' under the opposite bank. See! there is a good trout 'up' taking every may-fly that comes within half a dozen inches of his nose. He is lying almost against the clay side of the bank.

No, you were a little below him; you want a few more inches of line out. Now, that is right—let it go down; the fly is floating and sitting up on the water beautifully; he's got it—— Hurrah! Bring him down to that dry spot where I can get to the river with the net. . . . All right, I've got him. . . . Well, now, isn't he a beauty?—one of our genuine old Clear trout, and you will find that when cooked he is as pink as a salmon.

After lunch there is not often much doing on the Clear till the sun begins to get low and the shadow falls on the water, though here and there, while the fly is hatching at all, there is a good chance of picking up an odd fish or two. In certain cool and shady spots, under the willows, at the hatches, and by the small foot-bridge, a trout may very often be found rising more or less steadily all day at may-flies, duns, or spinners, and such a fish, being a well-fed, active fellow, affords the best of sport. Perhaps between five and seven is the cream of the day on this stretch of the Clear, as it is on many another stream. In the cool and quiet of the evening the bigger trout steal from their hiding-places and come to the surface for a change of diet.

Though the Clear is not one of those aggravating streams only good in the may-fly season, it certainly contains heavy trout that rarely stir at surface food at any other time, and to overcome one of these rare risers is a triumph second surely to few in the world

A Visit to Troutbridge

of English sport. The first rush of the salmon is imperial; and a thrill of delight will seldom be wanting when the sportsman brings down cleverly the one woodcock of the day, or scores with a difficult right and left on the first of September. But let me handle the ten-foot rod bent double by a three-pound trout in perfect condition in may-fly time! I know of no sporting sensation equal to it.

By seven o'clock the hatch of fly and the rise of trout seem to be over for the day. Not a solitary may-fly is to be seen where there were scores sailing down stream and fluttering out into the fields an hour since: and the stream is as a fishless one; not a single trout even of the sprat size can be espied near the surface. 'No more good to-day!' you who know not the beauty and the glamour of the Clear as the still June night draws in, may exclaim. Perhaps you have scruples against angling in the semi-darkness, or more likely have ordered dinner at the inn for eight o'clock sharp.

Well, never mind the dinner. The steak can be kept hot somehow, and as for pudding, why, did not Shelley say that pudding was a prejudice? I have often, when angling, failed to get back in time for dinner, and have never regretted it.

In this evening time the Clear has wondrous beauties unknown to those who only see her crystalline streams by broad daylight; while a certain mystery lurks in her deeper pools and oily-looking swirls among the rough old willow-trees. If a trout be found moving here now, it will take much to convince you that it is not a very big fellow indeed. It is possible that in the deep backwater at Wild Duck Corner—they say it is as much in low water as seventeen feet—you will come upon and slay the traditional eight-pounder of the Clear. He was seen moving last year on just such another evening, taking everything he could find at the surface of the great black pool; the water-keeper watched him for some time, and was convinced he would have taken at once had there been

A Visit to Troutbridge

a rod on the spot. No angler worthy the name will leave for the sake of mere dinner the banks of the Clear while there is yet a chance in the fading light of even getting broken in a fish which has long been one of the glories of Troutbridge.

CHAPTER XXI

A Purist amongst Purists

MANY all-round anglers, and even some enthusiastic fly-fishermen, used to think the man was really too much of the purist, that he quite overdid the thing. At the bare mention of a minnow, or artificial spinning bait of any kind, he turned up his eyes in pious horror; and to resort to the worm under any conditions—even if the custom of the

A Purist amongst Purists

river warranted and even encouraged it—was, in his eyes, simple sacrilege. No, nothing but the driest of dry flies would he approve of, or allow to be really scientific angling, and the wet-fly angler on a chalk stream he regarded as an abomination, an anachronism. 'It may be magnificent,' he would say, in somewhat acid tones, 'getting a basket of heavy trout with a sunk fly, but it is not fishing.' Others might do it, if so they chose, on those streams, at any rate, which were not absolutely sacred to the proper scientific method; but, for his own part, he would rather put up his rod and never cast a fly again than adopt 'chuck and chance it' tactics. 'For those who like that sort of thing, it's just the sort of thing they like,' was another favourite saying of his in regard to anglers practising the wet-fly as well as dry-fly method.

He had no patience whatever with his friend All-Rounder, who for a long while frequented the same good old hostelry in the north country, and who himself preferred dry-fly fishing, but did not hesitate to put a large sunk alder, or even a small Jock Scott, over a tailing trout; and used to go the length of denying that trout captured by such means ought to be counted in the day's bag of the true scientific angler. This purist was never tired of laying stress on what he called 'the real thing,' namely, taking a 'fair rising trout' with a single small fly; he objected to may-fly fishing, and regarded it as a base slaughter—even when dry and floating for all the world like the natural insect. He would sometimes say, when showing you, with it may be the reluctance born of modesty, the contents of his creel, ' Ah, I can scarcely count that trout, because the brute actually took the fly after it had commenced to drag'; or else, 'Well, I'm afraid no credit attaches to me in regard to that fish, because I did not actually cast to it, but to another fish a foot away.' He made a golden rule of never fishing a likely-looking spot—even with the driest of floating flies—on chance; and, though he would sometimes

A Purist amongst Purists

try a likely-looking trout lying obviously on the look-out for food near the surface, he professed to take but little pride and interest in such an operation; it was not quite 'the real thing.' Of course, a good many keen and good anglers hold somewhat similar views, but this one would somehow be for ever forcing them upon you. It was his solemn boast that as a scientific angler he was *sans peur et sans reproche*. His friends, therefore, could not but admit that he was—though a good fellow and a fairly good angler—a bit of a purist, whilst his enemies called him a prig; possibly something in between the two would have hit him off to a nicety—say a purist amongst purists.

On days when nothing was doing, and no fly hatching, he might not rarely be heard remarking that he had not wetted his line. When he came back to the angling inn with nothing in his creel, which was often the case, as it is often the case, for the matter of that, with ninety-nine anglers out of a hundred, he did not go in for a number of lame excuses, but commonly remarked that he had found no trout rising at the fly. If his critic and opponent, Pot-hunter, had a basketful, he would contrive to let the company know that they were not killed in the orthodox scientific style. Once he and Stripling were left alone at the angling inn at the end of the summer holidays, and, as may be imagined, the latter got many lectures on 'the real thing,' and how it should be achieved. Stripling knew nothing about fly-fishing, but was eager to learn, and was so greatly interested when the purist told him how to sit still and watch for rising trout, if necessary by the hour, that he resolved to thoroughly master the mysteries of the art. Accordingly, one soft September evening he crouched down in the tall and thick river herbage close to a spot famed for heavy trout, content, if need be, to wait and to watch for a couple of hours or so. The following is what, after a while, he saw, open-mouthed: the purist cautiously making his way to the river-side through a bed of osiers, all eyes and ears, as though apparently

A Purist amongst Purists

he as little desired to be seen by human beings as by trout; the purist, having arrived at the water-side, select a spot where the stream ran deep and rather sluggish; the purist take a small tin case out of his breast-pocket, impale a writhing worm, secreted in the moss in that case, on his hook, and forthwith hurriedly and rather guiltily commit 'simple sacrilege.' The Stripling, being wise, held his peace; but when in the smoking-room that same evening he listened to yet another lecture on the usual subject, he could not help thinking that there was more in 'the real thing,' as carried out by his new friend the purist, than appeared on the surface.

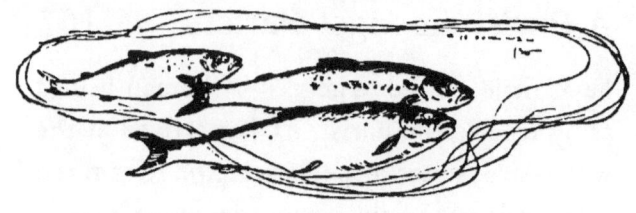

CHAPTER XXII

On a Hampshire Common

NEITHER the angler nor the gunner in the course of his sporting expeditions can often in the British Isles come upon a spot richer in bird, flower, and insect life than Bransbury Common in the delicious valley of the Test. It fell to my lot to spend three or four days there during the may-fly season—glorious days of crowded life indeed they were—and the spirit of the collector and naturalist could not but assert itself now and again at the expense of the angler. Bransbury Common is a wild and marshy tract of some hundreds of acres, lying in the midst of a delightfully wooded, undulating, and very smiling district of north-west Hampshire. Close by, at well-named Longparish, the famous old sporting worthy, Colonel Hawker, throve during the first half of the century, and the country is still a thoroughly sporting one. In may-fly time you will notice at the entrance of almost every little inn you pass hereabouts implements of the angle, such as wading-stockings or trousers, fishing-baskets, and many a rod with gut cast fluttering in the breeze. Game, too, is still plentiful, both furred and feathered. I think that if the sturdy Colonel could but return to his well-loved haunts to-day, he would find things not altered so very greatly for the worse, though, perhaps, he would be a little scandalised at the conduct of the trout if he angled for them with his old cast of flies. The old thatched cottages, many of them containing the stout beams which tell of a day when bricks and mortar were still something of a luxury in such out-of-the-world parts, must be much the same as they were in his time, and their gardens must be growing much the same herbs and old-fashioned blooms; nor do the red-brick farmhouses and great farmyards bear signs of considerable change. The scythe has to some extent been superseded, as has the good old hand-driven plough, and there is a railway station at Longparish—a very pretty one, be it added; but other changes are probably neither numerous nor material. Bransbury Common itself is as untouched by civilising influences as Exmoor Forest. It is the weird haunt, as I discovered to my delight, of the skulking water-rail, the drumming snipe—that quaint little bird, all 'belly and bill,' as Mr. Emerson calls it—of the beautiful cotton-sedge, of the marsh fritillary butterfly, of the pink underwing moth, and last, but to the angler-naturalist assuredly not least, of the most splendid trout. The Common is watered by three streams, the Test proper, the 'Old River,' and the 'Small River,' as well as by several springs and feeders. I came upon the fritillary, an insect which many ardent entomologists are never fortunate enough to observe in a wild state, while I was stalking a golden-hued, crimson-spotted trout in the

On a Hampshire Common

'Small River' up to the knees in water, and it made me forget all about angling for a few minutes; for there are few sensations more pleasurable than that of the collector who sees for the first time on the wing a scarce or local insect which he has long coveted. *Artemis* is possibly not the only interesting butterfly to be found on Bransbury in due season, but at the time I was there I saw nothing else except small-heaths and orange-tips.

The Common boasts many elegant, refreshing, and interesting plants. Of the orchises, which grew in the greatest profusion, I noticed the early, the spotted, and the fragrant. The last-named derives its specific name, *Conopsea*, from its somewhat fanciful resemblance to the family of insects called *Conops* by Linnæus. The resemblance is not so good as that of the odd green-man orchis, which grows in fair quantity in some of the neighbouring Hampshire woods, and has the comical appearance of a naked figure; nor as that of the bee-orchis. Ragged-robin, of course, flourishes everywhere on this marshy place; so does the buck-bean and the grass of Parnassus. These, however, were only a few of the bright and sweet plants which our nosegays each day contained. Here and there on the Common are patches of the glossy, silken cotton-sedge; close to the river's brink, the yellow iris; on the higher ground, wild-roses and honeysuckle in any quantity.

But the bird life of Bransbury Common is, perhaps, the really most attractive feature of all. Scores of lapwings perpetually wheel about, uttering their mournful notes by day, and often, when the moon is up, by night too; you are constantly flushing snipe; and in one corner of the Common, which the village children cannot reach owing to the depth of the boggy water, a small colony of wild-ducks bring up their broods in security. By a little creek I disturbed a party. The male bird, though obviously concerned on behalf of his family, withdrew expeditiously; whilst the female, after feigning to be hurt in a manner that struck me as decidedly overdone, returned

On a Hampshire Common   173

and fluttered about almost within reach of my nine-foot rod. Presently I came upon the young, who were well able to look after themselves; they fled across the river in a long line, with swiftness and decision, their mother clamorously bringing up the rear, and seeming almost to push some of them into the rushes on the opposite bank. It was all so unnecessary! The water-rail sometimes resorts to the same device of feigning to be injured. One which I flushed close to the road in a very boggy spot deceived me for a few seconds. She had a nest close at hand, I felt sure, in one of the great firm 'mats,' as the country-people call the tufts of dry grass in the marsh; but I searched in vain. The water-rail brings up, it is stated, two broods every season. It is very pleasant to find this bird so much at home, and so almost abundant, by the Test—I flushed three in one day—for it is getting terribly scarce, even in some of its strongholds and watery fastnesses. 'I believe,' writes an authority on bird life in the Broads, 'that the water-rail will one day be as rare in the Broads district as the spotted crake is to-day.' The poor, nervous, diffident creature has enemies enough and to spare without man molesting it. Long may the water-rail find a safe abiding-place in the valley of the Test! It is not, I am glad to say, by any means peculiar to Bransbury Common and district. Mr. Stewart, in his 'Birds of our Country,' mentions having seen the bird by the Test, and having found its nest and eggs on one occasion. Four members of the family *Rallidæ* I found at Bransbury and in the district during my few days' sojourn there; and I cannot help thinking that a fifth, the spotted crake, may occasionally find a secure home in the Test valley during the breeding season.

Printed by T. and A. CONSTABLE, Printers to Her Majesty
at the Edinburgh University Press

www.ingramcontent.com/pod-product-compliance
Lightning Source LLC
Chambersburg PA
CBHW031440160426
43195CB00010BB/797